BIG BOOK OF KNITTED SOCKS

JORID LINVIK'S

Big book of

KNITTED
SOCKS

45 DISTINCTIVE SCANDINAVIAN PATTERNS

Trafalgar Square
North Pomfret, Vermont

First published in the United States of America
in 2017 by
Trafalgar Square Books
North Pomfret, Vermont 05053

Originally published in Norwegian as *Den store sokkeboka*.

ISBN: 978-1-57076-842-2

Library of Congress Control Number: 2017947930

Interior Design and Layout: Johanna Hjorthol
Photography: Marthe Mølstre
Translation: Carol Huebscher Rhoades

Printed in China

10 9 8 7 6 5 4 3 2 1

CONTENTS

PREFACE

When I was a child in the 1960s, everyone wore thick, hand-knitted socks during the winter. We called them *lesta*.

Winter boots and ski boots had to be big enough to fit a couple of good socks inside. If the shoes were too tight, the cold came creeping in because there had to be enough room for the air to circulate and hold in the heat.

When we went inside, shoes and boots were always taken off and lined up in the entryway, as was, and still is, the custom all over the Nordic countries. It was considered rude to clomp in onto a clean floor with your outdoor footwear on! Also, in school, the boots stood in the entry hall because the floors in the class-rooms were sparkling clean. All the kids sat in their seats with their homemade knitted socks on their feet.

Every home had a wood-burning stove in the living room and sometimes also in the kitchen, but the rest of the house was often without heating. Wool socks were not taken off before you crept into the nice, warm comforter in the evening—and wool socks were the first thing you grabbed in the morning before setting your feet down on the ice-cold floor.

Sock knitting was considered, for the most part, women's work. That was an old and long-standing tradition, but it still held true. It almost counted as laziness if you just sat down with your hands in your lap. *Lest* or sock knitting was every-where, whether you went visiting, went to the women's association, or sat down to afternoon coffee. Only on Sundays was knitting put aside.

Sock yarn was usually gray, and spun with the coarsest and longest wool because that was the strongest. For extra decoration, the socks might, in the best case, have a few rounds in a color other than gray at the top of the leg. I was an adult before I realized that not only sweaters and cardigans but also socks could be embellished with different colors and patterns.

Since then, pattern knitting has completely taken hold of me! What could be better than a pair of new pattern-knitted socks in lovely colors, with a pretty motif?

In this book, you'll find 45 sock patterns, everything from completely easy to more advanced designs. The easy socks, knitted with only one strand of yarn per round, are based on traditional designs I've adapted for pattern socks.

My hope is that you'll enjoy this book for a long time and find patterns that keep your feet warm—and delight and inspire you.

So settle in and get cozy with loads of knitting!

Bodø, Norway
August 2016
Jorid Linvik

BASIC KNITTING TIPS

Ribbing

The ribbing at the top of the sock leg helps keep the sock in place so it won't sag down, and should be both firm and elastic. You should work the ribbing on needles one size smaller than the rest of the sock. You should also work the ribbing in proportion to the leg circumference of the person who will wear the socks.

Dominant Color

Most designs with two colors have a defined motif against a background. In the owl socks, for example, the owl is the motif. In order to have the smoothest possible results and make sure the motif will show clearly, it's important to hold the yarns the same way throughout. The motif or pattern yarn is knitted so that it comes under the other yarn on the back of the work. If you knit with a color in each hand, the motif strand should be in the left hand. If you hold both yarns over your left forefinger, the motif yarn should be held a little further down on that finger.

The two colors should be held at the same tension throughout the work. If they change places, the fabric will be uneven.

In the chart symbol keys for the patterns, the motif color is always the symbol on the left.

Wrong Side

To obtain a fine and evenly knitted sock, it's a good idea to check frequently that all "floats" lie evenly and smoothly on the wrong side. Tight strands between color changes mean the work will pull in across its width. Strands that are too loose are also a problem.

One tip is to stretch the stitches out across the width every time you change needles and to check the wrong side closely to make sure the strands lie flat and even.

Long Floats Between Color Changes

Long floats between color changes can be challenging and it's never good when there are loose strands inside the sock, waiting to catch on a toe! To avoid this, after every 5 or 6 stitches, twist the strands around each other on the wrong side. Stretch the piece carefully so the strands won't pull in.

Splicing Yarns

If you're in the middle of a row and the yarn has run out, you need to start with a new ball. You can tie the yarn ends with a loose knot and knit so the knot lands on the wrong side. Don't forget to leave ends long enough to weave in later on. When you've finished the piece, untie the knot and weave in the ends.

Uneven Yarn

Whenever you find knots, poor joins, or any other unevenness in the yarn, I recommend you cut out the bad spot and make a knot as described above. You'll regret not splicing the yarn if you just let it be.

Duplicate Stitch

Some of the patterns in the book have motifs that require duplicate stitch with a different color yarn over a few stitches in the design.

You can also use duplicate stitch in the same color yarn as the stitch(es) if, after the sock is finished, you discover a mistake on a stitch or two.

And you can always embellish socks even more with contrast color duplicate stitch, to add a personal touch.

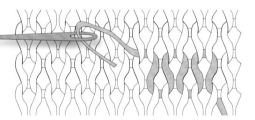

Duplicate stitch

Weaving in Yarn Ends

All yarn ends must be carefully woven in using a blunt tapestry needle on the wrong side of the sock.

First, check to make sure all yarn ends are pulled through to the wrong side so the right side is smooth.

Weave in ends by sewing them diagonally through the knitting for about 1½-2 in / 4-5 cm, going in and out through the tops of the stitches or through the strands in the stitch loops. Turn and sew back until a little past the starting point. Make sure the needle goes through the same strand you are sewing with a couple of times, and that the yarn lies smoothly without pulling in the fabric before you trim the end.

Sometimes you'll find little holes in the knitting—for example, at the junction of the heel and foot. You can tighten these holes on the wrong side at the same time as you weave in the ends. Use an end already at the hole or add a new strand of yarn.

Never tie knots in knitted fabric except as a provisional solution before you weave in ends. If you join ends with a knot only and the knot unties later on, there's no easy option for repairing the hole.

Joining with Kitchener Stitch

Some socks need to be seamed at the heel or toe using Kitchener stitch. Here's how to work the stitch:

Place the sets of stitches to be joined on separate needles. Sew through the stitches as shown in the drawing below, keeping the stitches on the needles until you can slip each off one by one as you complete the sewing through the stitch.

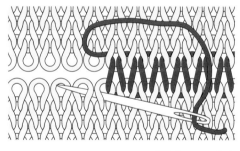

Kitchener stitch

If you make a mistake and the error is obvious, rip back and start over. Ripping back is frustrating and takes time, but it can often take just as much time to adjust a pattern to compensate for a mistake.

Wash and steam press the socks gently before you wear them or give them away.

YARN

The patterns for the socks in this book should be knitted with the chosen yarn type from well-known producers that sell yarn all around the country. Of course, you can choose exactly the yarn you want—just make sure it's suitable for the project you want to knit.

For socks, it's a good idea to choose a yarn that's reinforced one way or another and is extra-strong. That way, the socks will last a long time without getting any holes in the sole! Reinforced yarn is often spun of long-fibered wool and blended with synthetic fiber—for example, nylon. Your local yarn store can give you good advice about which yarns will be best for socks.

I've divided the sock yarns used for the patterns in this book into three basic categories:

BABY YARN

For the smallest socks, you can use fine baby yarn of whatever quality you like. Babies seldom wear out their socks, so you don't need to worry about using reinforced yarn.

FINE SOCK YARN

You have many different choices of quality and colors here.

The recommended gauge should be 25-30 stitches in 4 in / 10 cm.

HEAVY SOCK YARN

You also have a choice of quality and colors.

The recommended gauge should be 22-24 stitches in 4 in / 10 cm.

YARN SUPPLIERS

Dale Garn North America
www.dalegarnnorthamerica.com

Nordic Fiber Arts
www.nordicfiberarts.com

Swedish Yarn Imports
www.swedishyarn.com

Webs – America's Yarn Store
75 Service Center Road
Northampton, MA 01060
800-367-9327
www.yarn.com
customerservice@yarn.com

LoveKnitting.com
www.loveknitting.com/us

If you are unable to obtain any of the yarn used in this book, it can be replaced with a yarn of a similar weight and composition. Please note, however, the finished projects may vary slightly from those shown, depending on the yarn used. Try www.yarnsub.com for suggestions.

For more information on selecting or substituting yarn, contact your local yarn shop or an online store; they are familiar with all types of yarns and would be happy to help you. Additionally, the online knitting community at Ravelry.com has forums where you can post questions about specific yarns. Yarns come and go so quickly these days and there are so many beautiful yarns available.

GAUGE

The gauge determines the size of the finished socks. Simply put, gauge affects the size of every single stitch. Since the gauge of each individual stitch isn't easy to measure, gauges specify how many stitches there should be in 4 inches / 10 centimeters of knitting. This can also be a little tricky to measure, particularly on small knitted pieces with only a few stitches. Because knitting is elastic, it's difficult to measure precisely.

Lay the knitting down as flat as possible and place a ruler or measuring tape on top of it. Count the number of stitches in 4 in / 10 cm. The count that you get is the gauge.

Everyone's gauge will be a little different. Some knit loosely while others knit more tightly. It's difficult and usually unnecessary to adopt a knitting style other than the one you already have established. If you're one of those who knit tightly, you may want to use bigger needles than those recommended in the pattern; if you knit loosely, change to smaller needles.

Gauge and Stranded Two-Color Pattern Knitting
When you're knitting patterns with two colors, the gauge will be tighter than if you're knitting in stockinette with only one color. Based on the count given on the yarn ball band, you should add 2 extra stitches for every 4 in / 10 cm if you're knitting a multi-color pattern. The gauge also depends on the pattern itself, because a pattern with long floats between the color changes won't work at the same gauge as one with only one or two stitches between each color change. If you pull the yarn too much on the wrong side of the piece, the gauge will become even tighter.

HERE'S HOW TO PRODUCE THE RIGHT SIZE FOR THE SOCKS YOU WILL KNIT

① Find a pattern that can be knitted in the size you want.
② Decide on the gauge you need for the desired pattern.
③ Find a yarn marked with the same gauge. Calculate 2 extra stitches in gauge if working a two-color stranded pattern.

④ Choose needles that are a suitable size for the yarn. Recommended needle sizes are also given on yarn ball bands, but there's some wiggle room here and you might have to adjust it.
⑤ Knit a swatch big enough for you to measure the gauge. If it's too tight, change to larger needles; if it's too loose, try smaller needles.

All the socks in this book can be knitted in different sizes, even if there's only one size given. Consider, for example, these Let's Rock socks. The large pair to the right corresponds to men's shoe size U.S. 13 / Euro 46, and was worked with Sterk (CYCA #3, DK) from Du Store Alpakka on U.S. 4 / 3.5 mm needles. The socks to the left were knitted with the same pattern but using U.S. 1.5 / 2.5 mm needles and Nordlys (CYCA #1, fingering) yarn from Viking. They correspond to women's size U.S. 6 / Euro 36-37.

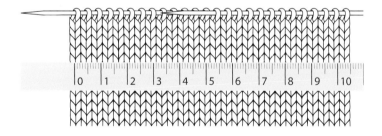

It's a good idea to write down the results of your gauge swatch to make it easier the next time. When you become more experienced, you'll be able to look at a pattern and know what yarn and needle size you can probably use for it.

SIZING AND MEASUREMENTS

All the socks in this book can be knitted in several sizes, depending on your yarn choice and needle size. In addition, you can also adjust the foot length for most of the patterns so they'll fit the person who will wear them more precisely.

It's a good idea to have a pair of socks that fit well at hand so you have something to measure against as you work. If you're knitting for someone who isn't nearby, you can ask the recipient to draw an outline of their foot on a piece of paper and send it to you. It's so frustrating to knit socks that turn out to be too small or too big!

The table to the right shows the length (as measured from heel to toe) for the foot in relation to U.S. and European shoe sizes.

Foot Circumference

The circumferences of both the leg and foot vary from person to person. Luckily, knitted garments are elastic, particularly across the width. But if you stretch them out too much widthwise, that will shorten the length. A sock might start off the right length but become too short on the foot because the foot is wide. If you want socks with extra width in the legs, work the legs on larger needles.

SHOE SIZES		FOOT LENGTH	
U.S.	EURO	INCHES	CENTIMETERS
Toddler 4½	20	4¾	12
Toddler 5½	21	5	12.5
Toddler 6½	22	5¼	13.5
Toddler 7	23	5½	14
Toddler 8	24	6	15
Toddler 9	25	6 1/8	15.5
Toddler 9½	26	6¼	16
Toddler 10	27	6½	16.5
Child 11	28	6¾	17
Child 11½	29	7	18
Child 12½	30	7¼	18.5
Child 13½	31	7½	19
Child 1	32	7 7/8	20
Child 2	33	8	20.5
Child 3	34	8½	21.5
Women's 4½	35	8¾	22
Women's 5½	36	8¾	22.5
Women's 6½	37	9¼	23.5
Women's 7½	38	9½	24
Women's 8½/ Men's 6	39	9 5/8	24.5
Women's 9½/ Men's 7	40	10	25.5
Women's 10½ / Men's 8	41	10¼	26
Women's 11½ / Men's 9	42	10½	26.5
Men's 10	43	10¾	27.5
Men's 11	44	11¼	28.5
Men's 12	45	11½	29
Men's 13	46	11¾	30

HOW TO FOLLOW THE CHARTS IN THE BOOK

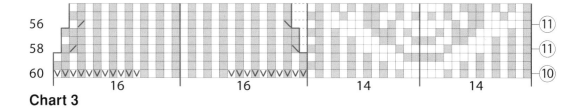

Chart 3

A number within a circle corresponds to the same number for a step in the pattern and refers to the round indicated by the arrow.

Marked vertical lines on the chart indicate the division of stitches on the needles, to make it easier to follow the pattern. If you're knitting on a circular, you can place markers at each vertical line on the chart.

The numbers between the red lines at the bottom of the chart show the stitch count for each needle.

The numbers at the left side of the chart show the total number of stitches on the round.

All increases are marked with a V.

The marked square is the "new" stitch. The stitches are worked in the color of the square.

Increases can be made in several ways:

M1 = make one—lift the strand between two stitches and knit into the back loop. The yarn that's lifted up should be the same color as the yarn color for that stitch.

OR

RLI = right-lifted increase—insert the tip of the right needle into the stitch below the one on the needle and bring yarn through. Knit the stitch on the left needle.

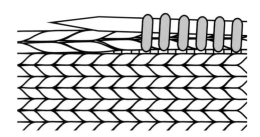

Picking up and knitting new stitches along the edge of the heel flap.

Every new stitch that will be picked up along an edge is marked with the same symbol, a V.

More stitches are always picked up

along the side edge than the number of stitches in the length of the heel. Try to pick up stitches as evenly spaced as possible.

Decreases are indicated by a diagonal line in the square where the decrease occurs. For each decrease, there will be one stitch less on the round—shown by a "notch" at the side of the chart.

◩ Right-leaning Decrease
◪ Left-leaning Decrease

The chart will indicate whether a decrease should lean to the right or left. Right-leaning Decrease = Knit 2 stitches together.
Left-leaning Decrease = Knit 2 stitches together through back loops.

OR Slip 1, k1 through back loop, pass slipped st over;
OR Ssk = (Sl 1 knitwise) 2 times and then knit the two stitches together through back loops
The pattern charts show which direction the decrease will lean. Several decreases stacked one over the other can form a ridge, in which case the decreases must all lean in the same direction so they'll match. If a single decrease comes in the middle of a row, it can be decreased in whichever direction you like.

Knitting back and forth

The heels on most of the socks in this book are worked back and forth. On the chart, read the right side rows from right to left and the wrong side rows from left to right.

Even if the chart is read from the opposite direction, when you are working on the wrong side, the purl stitches are drawn as purl and knit stitches as knit.

To obtain an even edge at the side, always slip the first stitch on every row when working back and forth.

▥ Slip 1 stitch

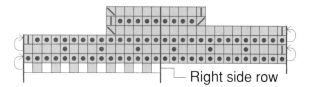

Right side row

ABBREVIATIONS

BO	bind off (= British cast off)	m	meter(s)	sl	slip
ch	chain st (crochet)	M1	make 1 = lift strand between two sts and knit into back loop	ssk	(sl 1 knitwise) 2 times and then knit together through back loops (left-leaning decease)
cm	centimeter(s)				
CO	cast on	mm	millimeter(s)		
dpn	double-pointed needles	p	purl		
		p2tog	purl 2 together	st(s)	stitch(es)
est	established	rem	remain(s)(ing)	tbl	through back loop(s)
in	inch(es)	rnd(s)	round(s)	WS	wrong side
k	knit	RS	right side	yd	yard(s)
k2tog	knit 2 together (right-leaning decrease)	sc	single crochet (= British double crochet)	yo	yarnover

PATTERN
INSTRUCTIONS

OLD-FASHIONED
BABY SOCKS

This is a very clear beginner's project that's easy to work. The socks are so sweet in all their simplicity, and invite extra decoration if you like. If you need ties for the socks, you can thread them between the stitches even if you haven't made eyelets.

As an introduction, just to warm up your needles, I want to show you a baby sock. This is a traditional pattern and probably the first one I learned to knit. The socks are nice and thick—just like slippers.

Materials

Yarn: CYCA #3 (DK/light worsted) Du Store Alpakka Sterk (40% Merino wool, 40% alpaca, 20% nylon; 150 yd/137 m / 50 g)
Needles: U.S. size 1.5 / 2.5 mm: straights
Crochet Hook: U.S. size B / 2.5 mm
Notions: 2 small rounded buttons

STITCHES

1 garter ridge = 2 rows of knit stitches.

k = knit
k2tog = knit two stitches together

INSTRUCTIONS

① CO 12 sts. Working back and forth, knit 12 ridges (= 24 rows).
② 13th ridge: K12 and then CO 12 new sts. Knit 24 more ridges (= 48 rows) with 24 sts across each row.

③ On the 12th ridge, BO the first 12 sts.
④ Knit 12 ridges over 12 sts. BO.
⑤ Foot edging: Change to another color. Pick up and knit 12 sts along each side and 8 sts at center front = 56 sts total. Knit 4 ridges back and forth over the 56 sts.

SOLE:

Change to a third color and knit 2 ridges.
On the 3rd ridge of the sole, k23, k2tog, k6, k2tog, knit to end of row. Knit 1 row without decreasing.
On the 4th ridge, K2tog, k21, k2tog, k4, k2tog, knit until 2 sts remain and end k2tog.
Knit 1 row without decreasing.
On the 5th ridge, k2tog, k20, k2tog, k2, k2tog, knit until 2 sts remain and end k2tog.
Knit 1 row.

FINISHING:

Join the 23 sts of each side under the sole together with Kitchener stitch. Seam the center back. Weave in all ends neatly on WS.

STRAP:

CO 14 sts with the same color as for the edge. Knit 2 ridges (4 rows) and then BO. Crochet a little loop on one end, making chain sts long enough to hold button well. Sew the other end of the strap to the edge of the sock. Make sure each strap lies correctly.

Sew a button to each sock. Make sure the buttons are very securely sewn on.

EDGING:

Crochet a little edging at the top of each sock. Work (2 sc + 1 ch) between every other ridge.

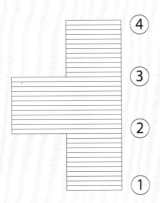

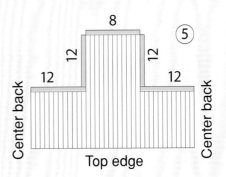

MAMA'S SOCKS

The starting point for all the socks in this first section are my mother's good old basic patterns. The first patterns are those she knitted and explained to me. After that are some with lovely designs, to make everyone—big and small—happy. All are based on the simple basic pattern with Mama's heel shaping.

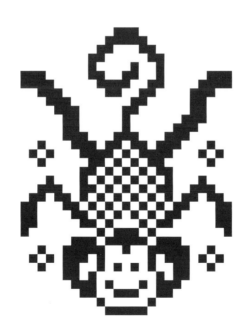

Basic Pattern for Mama's Socks

Sizes: Men's (Women's, Children's)

Gauge: 24 sts in stockinette = 4 in / 10 cm

Yarn Suggestions: The first three models are knitted with Sterk from Du Store Alpakka, CYCA #3 (DK/light worsted) (40% Merino wool, 40% alpaca, 20% nylon; 150 yd/137 m / 50 g)

Yarn Amounts for Single-Color Socks:

Men's sizes: 3 balls

Women's sizes: 2 balls

Children's sizes: about 1 ball

Needles: U.S. size 1.5 / 2.5 mm: set of 5 dpn

INSTRUCTIONS

CO 56 (48, 44) sts; distribute sts as evenly as possible over 4 dpn. Join, being careful not to twist cast-on row.

Work in k2, p2 ribbing (begin with k2) for 60 (54, 44) rounds.

The heel is worked back and forth in stockinette over half the total number of sts around. Place one half sts on a holder for the instep.

For Men's (Women's) sizes: Begin the row with one st before the beginning of the round so the edges of the heel will be aligned over the knit and purl sts of the ribbing.

Knit the next 28 (24, 22) sts and, *at the same time*, increase 4 sts evenly spaced across = 32 (28, 26) sts. Work back and forth in stockinette for 20 (18, 16) rows.

HEEL TURN:

Row 1: K20 (18, 17), k2tog tbl (or ssk); turn work.

Row 2: P9, p2tog; turn.

Row 3: K9, k2tog tbl (or ssk); turn.

Repeat Rows 2-3 until 10 heel sts rem. Cut yarn.

Foot: Begin at the left side of the heel flap.

Needle 1: Pick up and knit 10 (9, 8) sts along the heel flap. Knit the first 5 sts of the heel turn.

Needle 2: Knit the last 5 sts of heel turn and then pick up and knit 10 (9, 8) sts along opposite side of heel flap.

Needles 3-4: Knit the sts from the holder = instep. Continue in stockinette around and around: Knit 10 (9, 8) rnds. On the next rnd, decrease 1 st at each side of the sole. Usually the decreases are worked as: Knit until 3 sts rem on Ndl 2 (before the instep), k2tog, k1. Knit across instep and then, on Ndl 1 (after instep), k1, k2tog tbl (or ssk). Decrease the same way every 10 (9, 8) rnds until the stitch counts for the sole and instep are the same.

Continue for about another 15 (12, 8) rnds before the toe shaping. From the beginning of the toe shaping to the end is about 2¼ (1½, 1¼) in / 5.5 (4, 3.5) cm. Try the sock on and knit a bit more if necessary.

TOE SHAPING:

Begin over the instep:

Rnd 1: *K1, k2tog, knit until 3 sts rem on instep and then k2tog tbl (or ssk), k1*. Rep from * to * across the sole.

Rnd 2: Knit around.

Rep Rnds 1-2 until 6 or 8 sts rem. Join the sole and instep sts with Kitchener st.

Weave in all ends neatly on WS. Make the second sock the same way.

MAMA'S SOCKS
FOR HIM

The basic item in every man's wardrobe is a pair of good, hand-knitted socks. Anyone who goes out and about during the winter knows that wool socks will provide the right amount of warmth inside boots.

These socks are knitted in men's sizes following the Basic Pattern. They don't have to be gray, of course—everyone likes socks in bright colors!

MAMA'S SOCKS
FOR HER

The first sock is always more fun to knit than the second because the second one needs to have a matching row count so the socks will be exactly the same. If you knit in stripes, though, counting for the second sock is much easier. Stripes also liven up the socks and are a good way to use up some leftover yarn. If you want the socks to match exactly, it's a good idea to weigh that leftover yarn and divide it in half— that way you can be sure you have enough to work both socks the same way.

These socks are knitted following the women's size for the Basic Pattern.

After 10 rounds, work 3 rounds in a stripe color, then 3 rounds main color, 6 rounds stripe color, 3 rounds main color, 3 rounds stripe color. Continue with main color only. The heel and toe can be worked with the stripe color. At 6 rounds before the toe shaping begins, work 3 rounds stripe color and 3 rounds main color. Now work the toe with the stripe color.

MAMA'S SOCKS
FOR CHILDREN

Children like bright colors and will love these nice stripes. Of course, you can use as many colors as you want— and you can knit as many stripes as you want.

These socks are knitted in the children's size following the Basic Pattern. After 12 rounds, work 4 stripes with 3 rounds in each color and then knit 10 rounds with the main color to the heel flap. After 5 rounds of the foot, knit 3 three-round stripes with each color.

SHORT SOCKS
WITH FOLDED
CUFFS

Instead of the regular ribbing at the top of these socks, I made a wide facing that I folded to the wrong side. The facing is worked in a different color than the rest of the socks. These socks are more like slippers and are easy to pull onto your feet when the floor's cold. If you like to embroider, the folded cuff is ideal for some decorative embroidery.

Use the basic pattern for Mama's socks. The stitch count is the same, so choose the size you want.

Instead of the ribbing on the leg, knit a cuff.

Sizes: Men's (Women's, Children's)

Facing: CO 56 (48, 44) sts with the color you want for the facing. Divide the sts as evenly as possible onto 4 dpn and join, being careful not to twist cast-on row.

Knit 14 (13, 12) rnds.

Cut yarn and change colors. Knit 1 rnd and then purl 1 rnd (the purl round is the foldline). Knit 16 (15, 14) rnds.

Rnd 17 (16, 15): Knit. You can attach the cuff lining as you knit this round. Using a second set of dpn or a circular, pick up each st in the cast-on row and knit the two sets of sts together. If this is too difficult, simply wait and sew down the lining after the socks are done.

Now work the heel and foot as for the Basic Pattern for Mama's Socks.

PREEMIE
SOCKS

Here's a pattern for teeny tiny little socks. For those who have come into the world a little early, these socks knitted with soft wool or alpaca will be an invaluable help. The socks can be used later for dolls—or you can hang a pair as decorations on the Christmas tree or key rack.

Knit these socks with the softest baby yarn you can find, on U.S. size 1.5 / 2.5 mm needles.

Instructions:

LIGHT PINK SOCKS:

CO 24 sts. Divide the sts with 6 sts on each dpn; join.

Work 4 rounds of k1, p1 ribbing. Knit 18 rnds and then 4 rnds in k1, p1 ribbing.

HEEL FLAP:

Place the front 12 sts on a holder for the instep. Work the heel back and forth in stockinette over 12 sts. Always slip the first st of each row. After 4 rows in stockinette, shape heel as follows: Beginning on RS, k8, ssk. *Turn and p5, p2tog. Turn and k5, ssk. Repeat from * until 6 sts rem. Cut yarn.

FOOT:

Needle 1: Pick up and knit 3 sts along the left side of the heel flap, k3 from heel.
Needle 2: K3 from heel, pick up and knit 3 sts along right side of heel flap.
Needles 3-4: Knit the held instep sts.

Continuing in k1, p1 ribbing on the instep sts and in stockinette on the sole, work 12 rnds.

TOE:

Knit all sts around. Decrease on all rounds to shape the toe as follows: (K2tog, knit until 2 sts before opposite side of instep/sole, ssk) 2 times around. Repeat the decrease round until 4 sts rem. Cut yarn and draw end through rem sts; tighten. Weave in all ends neatly on WS.
Make a second sock the same way.

DARK PINK SOCKS:

Work as for the light pink socks but work the entire sock in k1, p1 ribbing—except for the heel stitches and the sole.

RED SOCKS:

Work as for the light pink socks but with only 4 rounds of stockinette in each leg.

MAMA'S SOCKS
FOR LITTLE FEET

Make a little friend happy with a pair of fine hand-knitted socks in a pretty pattern. Small socks are quick to knit and the rewards are great. Perhaps you'll earn a well-deserved hug as a thank-you.

SIZES
As a starting point, all these socks are the same size, because they're knitted with the same type of yarn and on the same needles. One ball of yarn in each color is all you'll need to knit a pair. You can adjust the foot length when you get to the toe shaping.

FOOT LENGTH	SHOE SIZE	YARN	NEEDLES	GAUGE IN 4 IN / 10 CM
U.S. 4¼-5¼ in	4½-7	Baby yarn	1.5	28-30 sts
Euro 11-13.5 cm	20-23		2.5 mm	
U.S. 5½-6¾ in	8-11½	Fine Sock	1.5-2.5	26-27 sts
Euro 14-17 cm	24-29		2.5-3 mm	
U.S. 7-7½ in	12½-1	Heavy Sock	1.5-2.5	24-25 sts
Euro 18-19 cm	30-32		2.5-3 mm	
U.S. 8-8½ in	2-4½	Heavy Sock	2.5-4	22-23 sts
Euro 20-21.5 cm	33-35		3-3.5 mm	

Most of the socks use a "half rib" (ribbing worked on alternate rows) for the heel and toe, which makes those parts tighter and more elastic so the socks will conform nicely around the foot.

THE KNITTING CLUB'S FAVORITE

MATERIALS

Yarn: CYCA #2 (sport/baby) Dale Garn Falk (100% wool; 116 yd/106 m / 50 g): 1 ball each Blue and White

Needles: U.S. size 2.5 / 3 mm: set of 5 dpn

Gauge: 24 sts = 4 in / 10 cm (very elastic).

Foot Length: 6-9¾ in / 15-25 cm. You can adjust the foot length just before the toe shaping.

It is easy to knit in social groups (though of course if you need to concentrate on a complicated knitted garment, you should work alone). These socks almost knit themselves. This simple pattern is easy to follow even when you're chatting at the coffee table. That's why this design is called the "Knitting Club's Favorite."

These socks are worked in pattern and ribbing throughout, which makes them both firmly knitted and elastic, so they'll fit the foot well. Instead of the usual ribbing at the top of the leg, there are a few rounds of stockinette to make a rolled edge.

Instructions:

① With White, CO 48 sts and divide sts evenly onto 4 dpn; join. Work following Chart 1, repeating the pattern around. The first round is repeated 5 times so that a rolled edge forms. The rounds begin at the side of the sock.

② Work the rounds marked by the encircled 2 on Chart 1 two times.

③ Continue by working Chart 2 for the heel flap: turn the piece, work back over the next 23 sts and then work back and forth in pattern. Place the 25 rem sts on a holder for the instep (you'll come back to these sts when the heel is finished).

④ **Heel Turn:** Sl 1, work 14 sts, ssk; turn.

⑤ Repeat the following two rows until 9 sts rem:
WS: Sl 1, p7, p2tog; turn.
RS: Sl 1, k7, ssk; turn.

⑥ Now work following Chart 3 for the foot.
Rnd 1: Pick up and knit 9 sts along left side of heel flap; k9 to center of heel; with a new dpn, knit 9 rem heel sts; pick up and knit 9 sts along right side of heel flap. Slip held sts to two dpn and work in pattern.

⑦ Continue following Chart 3, decreasing as shown.

⑧ **Toe Shaping:** With White only, knit until foot is desired length before toe shaping. The chart shows how the toe is shaped on every round. If you follow the chart, it is about 1½ in / 4 cm from the first round of decreases to the tip of the toe. If you decrease on every other round the shaping will be narrower, with about 3 in / 8 cm between the first decrease round and the tip of the toe.

⑨ Cut yarn and draw end through rem sts; tighten. Weave in all ends neatly on WS.

Make the second sock the same way.

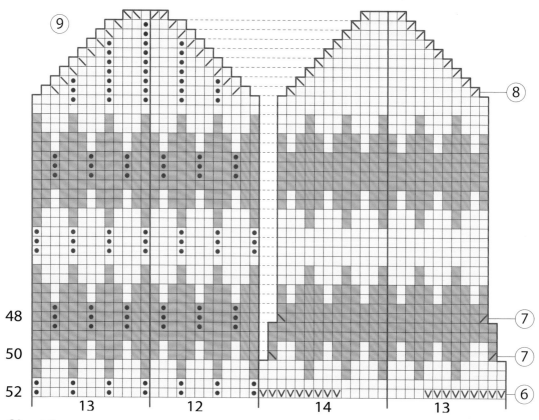

Chart 3

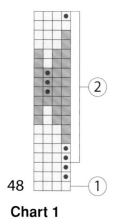

Chart 1

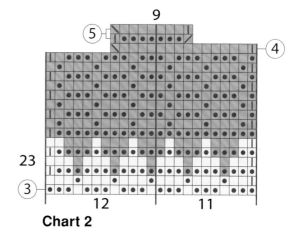

Chart 2

■	□	Knit
■	•	Purl
	☑	Increase 1 with M1
◩	☑	Right-leaning decrease
◪	◳	Left-leaning decrease
▥	▯	Sl 1

BABY OWLS

MATERIALS

Yarn: CYCA #3 (DK/light worsted) Du Store Alpakka Sterk (40% Merino wool, 40% alpaca, 20% nylon; 150 yd/ 137 m / 50 g): 1 ball each White and Charcoal; for the red stripes on the legs, use leftover yarn in a similar weight

Needles: U.S. sizes 1.5 and 2.5 / 2.5 and 3 mm: sets of 5 dpn

Foot Length: 7-10¼ in / 18-26 cm. You can adjust the foot length just before the toe shaping. These socks can be worked in several children's sizes (see the table at the beginning of this chapter).

These stylish little baby owls are hopping down from their secure nest for the first time ever because today is the first day of school. These easily knitted socks fit well on small feet and will inspire enthusiasm in anyone who is little and likes socks with pictures on them.

Instructions:

NOTE: You'll need two sets of double-pointed needles for these socks. Use the larger dpn for the sections with two-color stranded knitting and the smaller needles for the sections with only a single color.

① With smaller needles and Charcoal, CO 52 sts and divide sts evenly onto 4 dpn; join. The rounds begin at the center back of the sock. Work following Chart 1, repeating the pattern around. Work the first chart row in k2, p2 ribbing for 12 rounds and then work chevron pattern.

② At the encircled 2, increase 4 sts evenly spaced around = 1 st increased on each dpn = 56 sts. Change to larger needles.

③ At the encircled 3 at the top of Chart 1, work the k2, p2 ribbing for 15 rnds.

④ Continue by working Chart 2 for the heel flap: With Charcoal, knit 16 sts on the next rnd.

⑤ Turn and purl back = 30 sts. Place the 26 rem sts on a holder for the instep (you'll come back to these sts when the heel is finished). Do not cut yarn.

⑥ Work back and forth in stockinette for a total of 21 heel rows, ending with a WS row.

⑦ **Decrease:** Sl 1, k19, ssk; turn.

⑧ Repeat the following two rows until 12 sts rem, ending with a WS row:
WS: Sl 1, p10, p2tog; turn.
RS: Sl 1, k10, ssk; turn.

⑨ Now work following Chart 3 for the foot. Begin with the held instep sts: M1 before first st, k26; pick up and knit 10 sts along side of heel flap, k12 of heel; pick up and knit 10 sts along opposite side of heel flap. Continue working in the round.

⑩ Continue following Chart 3, decreasing at each side as shown.

⑪ Now work from Chart 4 for the toe shaping. The chart is repeated twice around. Repeat the first round until foot is desired length before toe shaping.

⑫ **Toe Shaping:** With White only, knit until foot is desired length before toe shaping. The chart shows how the toe is shaped on every round. If you follow the chart, it is about 1¼ in / 3 cm from the first round of decreases to the tip of the toe. If you decrease on every other round, the shaping will be narrower, with about 2½ in / 6 cm between the first decrease round and the tip of the toe.

⑬ Cut yarn and draw end through rem sts; tighten. Weave in all ends neatly on WS.

Make the second sock the same way.

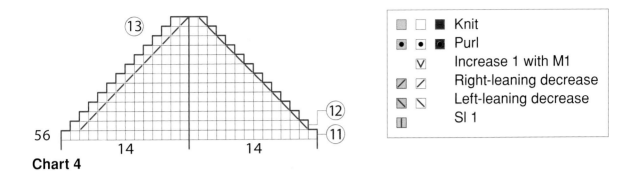

Chart 4

		Knit
•	•	Purl
	V	Increase 1 with M1
		Right-leaning decrease
		Left-leaning decrease
		Sl 1

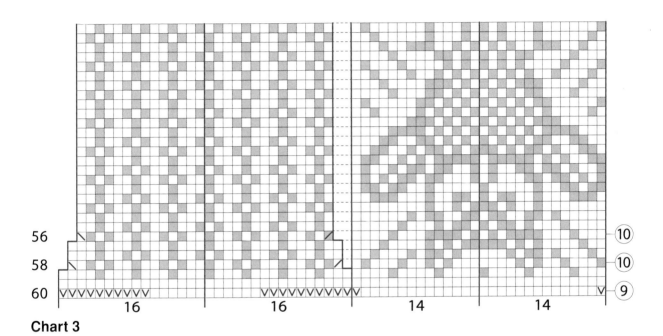

Chart 3

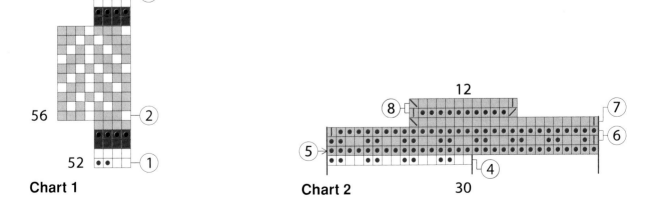

Chart 1

Chart 2

BABY PANDAS

MATERIALS

Yarn: CYCA #3 (DK/light worsted) Du Store Alpakka Sterk (40% Merino wool, 40% alpaca, 20% nylon; 150 yd/ 137 m / 50 g): 1 ball each White, Green, and Black

Needles: U.S. sizes 1.5 and 2.5 / 2.5 and 3 mm: sets of 5 dpn

Foot Length: 7-10¼ in / 18-26 cm. You can adjust the foot length just before the toe shaping. These socks can be worked in several children's sizes (see the table at the beginning of this chapter).

Everyone falls head over heels in love with baby pandas. These two little pandas are sitting patiently in the green grass, waiting for their mother. Maybe they'll get some little bamboo shoots as treats when she returns?

Instructions:

NOTE: You'll need two sizes of double-pointed needles for these socks. Use the larger dpn for the sections with two-color stranded knitting and the smaller needles for the sections with only a single color.

① With smaller dpn and Green, CO 52 sts and divide sts evenly onto 4 dpn; join. The rounds begin at the center back of the sock. Work following Chart 1, repeating the pattern around. Repeat the first chart row with k2, p2 ribbing for 12 rounds and then work block pattern.

② At the encircled 2, increase 4 sts evenly spaced around = 1 st increased on each dpn = 56 sts. Change to larger needles.

③ Repeat the k2, p2 ribbing rnd at the top of Chart 1 for 15 rnds.

④ Continue by working Chart 2 for the heel flap: with White, knit 16 sts on the next rnd.

⑤ Turn and purl back with Green = 30 sts. Place the 26 rem sts on a holder for the instep (you'll come back to these sts when the heel is finished). Do not cut yarn.

⑥ Work back and forth in stockinette for a total of 21 rows, ending on WS.

⑦ **Decrease:** Sl 1, k19, ssk; turn.

⑧ Repeat the following two rows until 12 sts rem (ending with a WS row):
WS: Sl 1, p10, p2tog; turn.
RS: Sl 1, k10, ssk; turn.

⑨ Now work following Chart 3 for the foot. Begin with the held instep sts: M1 before first st, k26; with another dpn, pick up and knit 10 sts along side of heel flap, k6 of heel; with a new dpn, k6 of heel and pick up and knit 10 sts along opposite side of heel flap. Continue working in the round.

⑩ Continue following Chart 3, decreasing 1 st at each side as shown.

⑪ Now work from Chart 4 for the toe shaping. The chart is repeated twice around. Repeat the second round in ribbing until foot is desired length before toe shaping.

⑫ **Toe Shaping:** With Green only, knit until foot is desired length before toe shaping. The chart shows how the toe is shaped on every round. If you follow the chart, it is about 1¼ in / 3 cm from the first round of decreases to the tip of the toe. If you decrease on every other round, the shaping will be narrower, with about 2½ in / 6 cm between the first decrease round and the tip of the toe.

⑬ Cut yarn and draw end through rem sts; tighten. Weave in all ends neatly on WS.

Make the second sock the same way.

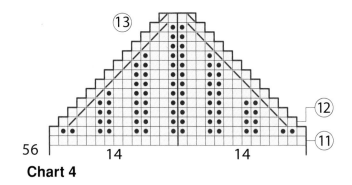

Chart 4

Knit key and charts:

- ■ □ □ Knit
- ⦁ ⦁ Purl
- Ⅴ Increase 1 with M1
- ⧄ ⧄ Right-leaning decrease
- ⧅ ⧅ Left-leaning decrease
- Ⅱ Sl 1

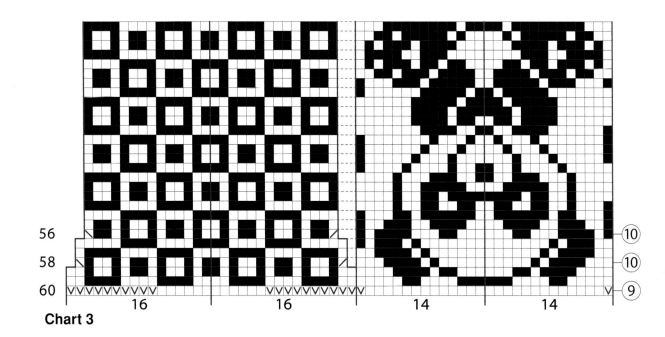

Chart 3

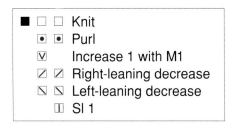

Chart 1

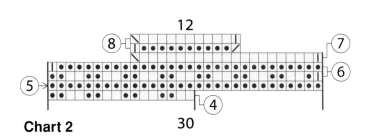

Chart 2

TIGER CUBS

MATERIALS

Yarn: CYCA #1 (sock/fingering/baby)
Rauma Baby Panda (100% wool; 191
yd/ 175 m / 50 g): 1 ball each Yellow
and Black

Needles: U.S. sizes 0 and 1.5 / 2 and
2.5: sets of 5 dpn

Foot Length: 5¼-6 in / 13.5-15 cm.
You can adjust the foot length just
before the toe shaping. These socks can be
worked in several children's sizes (see the table
at the beginning of this chapter).

Tigers are the largest and most dangerous
animals in the jungle. That's something the
little tiger cubs can completely rely on—even
if they aren't dangerous at all, only sweet
and nice, they can roar if they want.

Instructions:

NOTE: You'll need two sizes of double-pointed needles for these socks. Use the larger dpn for the sections with two-color stranded knitting and the smaller needles for the sections with only a single color.

① With smaller dpn and Yellow, CO 48 sts and divide sts evenly onto 4 dpn; join. The rounds begin at the center back of the sock. Work following Chart 1, repeating the pattern around. Repeat the first chart row with k1, p1 ribbing for 10 rounds.

② Work the rounds marked by the encircled 2 4 times.

③ Work from Chart 2 for the heel flap. Begin 13 sts before the beginning of the round; turn and purl 25.

④ Turn and work back and forth over 25 sts. Place the 23 instep sts on a holder (you'll come back to these sts when the heel is finished).

⑤ **Decrease:** Sl 1, k15, ssk; turn.

⑥ Repeat the following two rows until 9 sts rem (ending with a WS row):
WS: Sl 1, p7, p2tog; turn.
RS: Sl 1, k7, ssk; turn.

⑦ **Foot:** With larger needles, begin with picking up sts around the heel:
With Black, pick up and knit 12 sts along the left side of the heel flap, k9 of heel, pick up and knit 12 sts along opposite side of heel flap; work instep following Chart 3.
NOTE: The first 3 sts are the last 3 sts picked up and knitted along the heel. Divide the sts around to correspond to the counts below Chart 3.

Continue around until Chart 3 is completed.

⑧ Now work from Chart 4 for the toe shaping. The chart is repeated twice around. Knit the stripes with 2 rnds Black, 4 rnds Yellow. Knit until foot is desired length before toe shaping. The chart shows how the toe is shaped on every round. If you follow the chart, it is about 1 in / 2.5 cm from the first round of decreases to the tip of the toe. If you decrease on every other round, the shaping will be narrower, with about 2 in / 5 cm between the first decrease round and the tip of the toe.

⑨ Cut yarn and draw end through rem sts; tighten. Weave in all ends neatly on WS.

Make the second sock the same way.

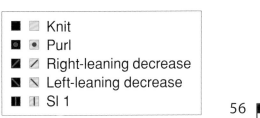

Knit
Purl
Right-leaning decrease
Left-leaning decrease
Sl 1

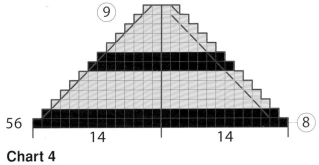

Chart 4

56   14   14   8   9

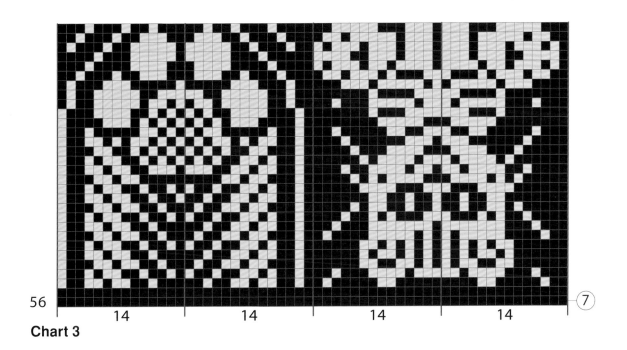

56   14   14   14   14   7

Chart 3

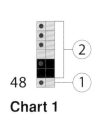

48   2   1

Chart 1

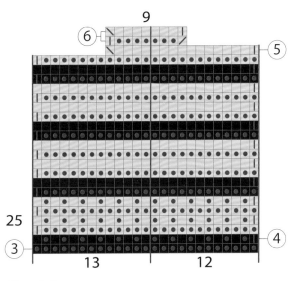

9

6   5

25   13   12   4

3

Chart 2

TRACTOR SOCKS

MATERIALS

Yarn: CYCA #2 (sport/baby) Trysil Garn Ida (80% wool, 20% nylon; 164 yd/ 150 m / 50 g): 1 ball each Yellow, Green, and Black

Needles: U.S. sizes 1.5 and 2.5 / 2.5 and 3 mm: sets of 5 dpn

Foot Length: 6¾ -9¾ in / 17-25 cm. You can adjust the foot length just before the toe shaping. These socks can be worked in several children's sizes (see the table at the beginning of this chapter).

Many children think heavy farm vehicles are fun. You can make a little one happy with a pair of good socks embellished with tractors. The wide tractor tracks function as panels around the top and bottom of the socks.

Instructions:

NOTE: You'll need two sizes of double-pointed needles for these socks. Use the larger dpn for the sections with two-color stranded knitting and the smaller needles for the sections with only a single color.

① With smaller dpn and Green, CO 52 sts and divide sts evenly onto 4 dpn; join. The rounds begin at the center back of the sock. Work following Chart 1, repeating the pattern around. Repeat the first chart row with k2, p2 ribbing for 12 rounds.

② At the encircled 2, increase 4 sts evenly spaced around = 1 st increased on each dpn = 56 sts. Change to larger needles.

③ Repeat these 4 rows (marked by the encircled 3) 5 times.

④ Continue by working Chart 2 for the heel flap: begin 16 sts before the round begins. Purl 29.
⑤ Turn and purl 29 with Yellow. Place the 27 rem sts on a holder for the instep (you'll come back to these sts when the heel is finished). Repeat these 2 rows at the encircled 5 until you've worked back and forth in stockinette for a total of 21 rows.

⑥ **Decrease:** Sl 1, k19, ssk; turn.

⑦ Repeat the following two rows until 12 sts rem (ending with a WS row):
WS: Sl 1, p9, p2tog; turn.
RS: Sl 1, k9, ssk; turn.

⑧ Now work following Chart 3 for the left foot and Chart 4 for the right foot.
Begin with the held instep sts: M1 before first st, k27; pick up and knit 11 sts along side of heel flap, k11 of heel; pick up and knit 10 sts along opposite side of heel flap. Continue working in the round.

⑨ Continue following respective Chart 3 or 4, decreasing 1 st at each side as shown.

⑩ Now work from Chart 5 for the left sock or Chart 6 for the right sock, repeating the pattern around.

⑪ Work from Chart 7 for the toe shaping. The chart is repeated twice around. With Yellow only, repeat the first round until foot is desired length before toe shaping.

⑫ **Toe Shaping:** The chart shows how the toe is shaped on every round. If you follow the chart, it is about 1¼ in / 3 cm from the first round of decreases to the tip of the toe. If you decrease on every other round, the shaping will be narrower, with about 2½ in / 6 cm between the first decrease round and the tip of the toe.

⑬ Cut yarn and draw end through rem 8 sts; tighten. Weave in all ends neatly on WS.

Make the second sock the same way, but make sure you follow the charts for the foot opposite the one you just knitted so the motifs will mirror each other.

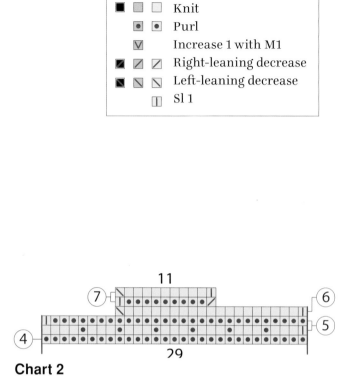

Knit
Purl
Increase 1 with M1
Right-leaning decrease
Left-leaning decrease
Sl 1

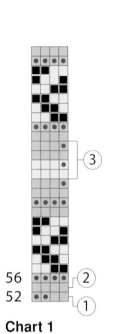

Chart 1

Chart 2

11

29

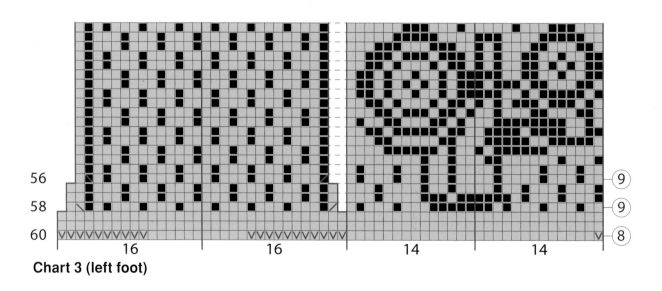

Chart 3 (left foot)

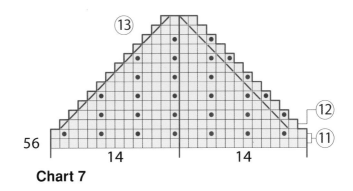

Chart 7

**Chart 5
(left foot)**

**Chart 6
(right foot)**

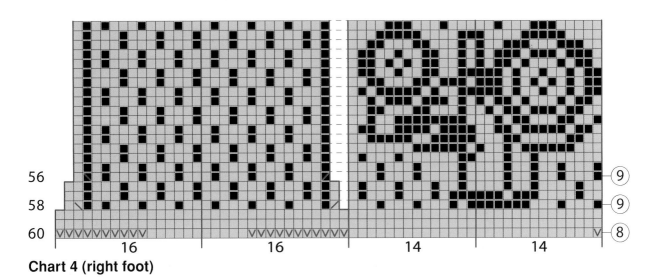

Chart 4 (right foot)

MONKEYS

MATERIALS

Yarn: CYCA #2 (sport/baby) Trysil Garn Ida (80% wool, 20% nylon; 164 yd/ 150 m / 50 g): 1 ball each Red-brown and White

Needles: U.S. sizes 1.5 and 2.5 / 2.5 and 3 mm: sets of 5 dpn

Foot Length: approx. 7 in / 18 cm. You can adjust the foot length just before the toe shaping. These socks can be worked in several children's sizes (see the table at the beginning of this chapter).

These good-natured monkeys climb high and low, swinging with their very long tails. Their smiling friends and public sit at the top of the leg.

Instructions:

NOTE: You'll need two sizes of double-pointed needles for these socks. Use the larger dpn for the sections with two-color stranded knitting and the smaller needles for the sections with only a single color.

① With smaller dpn and White, CO 48 sts and divide sts evenly onto 4 dpn; join. The rounds begin at the center back of the sock. Work following Chart 1, repeating the pattern around. Repeat the first chart row with k1, p1 ribbing for 8 rounds.

② Change to larger dpn. Increase 4 sts evenly spaced around = 1 st increased on each dpn = 52 sts.

③ At the encircled 3, increase 4 times as shown on the chart.

④ Work the stripe pattern at the encircled 4 for 10 rnds.

⑤ Now work from Chart 2 for the heel: Work 15 sts in stripe pattern.

⑥ Turn and purl 29. Place the 27 rem sts on a holder for the instep (you'll come back to these sts when the heel is finished).

⑦ Repeat these 2 rows (marked by the encircled 7) until you've worked back and forth in stockinette for a total of 21 rows (ending with a WS row).

⑧ **Decrease:** Sl 1, k19, ssk; turn.

⑨ Repeat the following two rows until 11 sts rem (ending with a WS row):
WS: Sl 1, p9, p2tog; turn.
RS: Sl 1, k9, ssk; turn.

⑩ Now work following Chart 3 for the left foot and Chart 4 for the right foot.

Begin with the held instep sts: M1 before first st, k27; pick up and knit 11 sts along side of heel flap, k11 of heel; pick up and knit 10 sts along opposite side of heel flap. Continue working in the round.

⑪ Continue following respective Chart 3 or 4, decreasing 1 st at each side as shown.

⑫ **Toe Shaping:** Decrease 2 sts at each side of foot as shown on the chart.

⑬ Join the sets of sole and instep sts with Kitchener st. Weave in all ends neatly on WS.

⑭ Make the second sock the same way, making sure you follow the charts for the foot opposite the one you just knitted so the monkeys mirror each other.

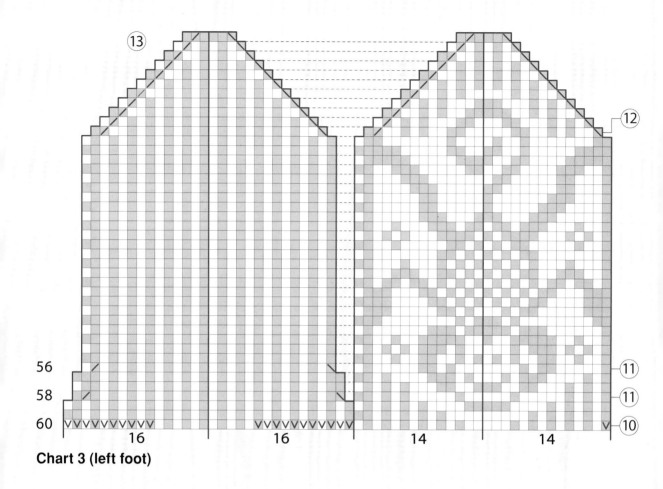

Chart 3 (left foot)

56
58
60

16   16   14   14

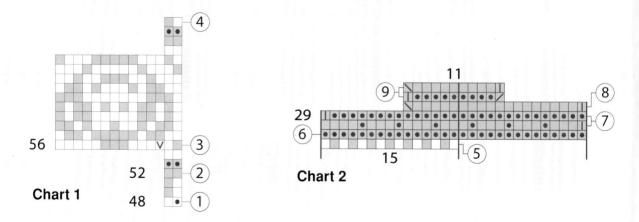

Chart 1

56
52
48

Chart 2

11
29
6
15

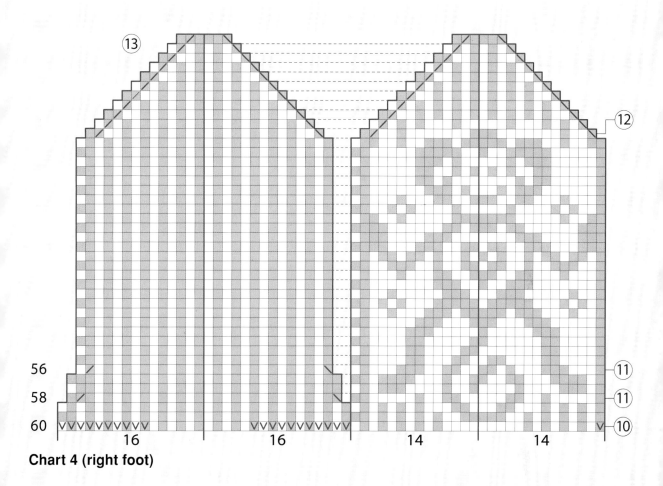

Chart 4 (right foot)

		Knit
		Purl
		Increase 1 with M1
		Right-leaning decrease
		Left-leaning decrease
		Sl 1

MAMA'S SOCKS
FOR BIGGER FEET

Pamper yourself with socks that suit your personality—or maybe you want to make a friend happy? All the socks are knitted on the same basic principles and you can pick and choose between several pretty designs.

SIZES

As a starting point, all of these socks are the same size, because they are knitted with the same type of yarn on the same needles.

For most of the socks, you can adjust the foot length when you get to the toe shaping.

FOOT LENGTH	SHOE SIZE	YARN	NEEDLES	GAUGE IN 4 IN / 10 CM
U.S. 8¾-9 in	5½-6½	Fine Sock	1.5	28-30 sts
Euro 22-23 cm	36-37		2.5 mm	
U.S. 9½-9¾ in	7½ -9½	Fine Sock	1.5-2.5	26-27 sts
Euro 24-25 cm	38-40		2.5-3 mm	
U.S. 10¼-10¾ in	10½-10*	Heavy Sock	2.5-4	24-25 sts
Euro 26-27 cm	41-43		3-3.5 mm	
U.S. 11-11 ¾ in	10*-13*	Heavy Sock	4-6	22-23 sts
Euro 28-30 cm	44-46		3.5-4 mm	

* *Men's size; all other sizes are women's*

Most of the socks use a "half rib" (ribbing worked on alternate rows) for the heel and toe, which makes those parts tighter and more elastic so the socks will conform nicely around the foot.

Choose yarn and needles that work well together to produce the gauge you want.

AFRICA

MATERIALS

Yarn: CYCA #1 (sock/fingering/baby) Viking of Norway Nordlys (75% wool, 25% nylon; 382 yd/ 349 m / 100 g): one 100 g ball each Black and multicolor #934

Needles: U.S. sizes 1.5 and 2.5 / 2.5 and 3 mm: sets of 5 dpn

Gauge: 27 sts = 4 in / 10 cm

Foot Length: You can adjust the foot length just before the toe shaping. These socks can be worked in several adult sizes (see the table at the beginning of this chapter).

The panels on these socks were inspired by traditional African patterns. Long socks with colorful pattern panels are always fun to knit—but that usually means there are many ends to weave in when you're finished. Here, you can "cheat"; we've used a multi-color yarn that makes the color changes all on its own.

Instructions:

NOTE: You'll need two sizes of double-pointed needles for these socks. Use the larger dpn for the sections with two-color stranded knitting and the smaller needles for the sections with only a single color.

① With smaller dpn and multi-color yarn, CO 68 sts and divide sts evenly onto 4 dpn; join. The rounds begin at the center back of the sock. Work following Chart 1, repeating the pattern around. Repeat the first chart row with k2, p2 ribbing for 12 rounds.

② Change to larger dpn. Increase 4 sts evenly spaced around = 1 st increased on each dpn = 72 sts.

③ On chart row marked with encircled 3, decrease 6 sts evenly spaced around = 66 sts rem.

④ On chart row marked with encircled 4, decrease 2 sts evenly spaced around = 64 sts.

⑤ Now work from Chart 2 for the heel: Cut yarn, turn work and begin 17 sts before the beginning of the round; purl 33.

⑥ Place the 31 rem sts on a holder for the instep (you'll come back to these sts when the heel is finished). Repeat the 2 rows at the encircled 6 until you've worked back and forth in stockinette for a total of 25 rows (ending with WS row).

⑦ **Decrease:** Sl 1, k20, ssk; turn.

⑧ Repeat the following two rows until 11 sts rem (ending with a WS row):
WS: Sl 1, p9, p2tog; turn.
RS: Sl 1, k9, ssk; turn.

⑨ Now work following Chart 3 for the foot. Pick up and knit 16 sts along left side of heel flap, k11 of heel; pick up and knit 16 sts along opposite side of heel flap, and then work the 31 held sts of instep. Continue working in the round.

⑩ Decrease 1 st at each side on every other round as shown on the chart.

⑪ Decrease 1 st at each side as indicated on the chart.

⑫ Decrease 1 st at each side as shown on the chart.

⑬ Now work following Chart 4 for the toe shaping. The chart is repeated two times around. Repeat the first 2 rounds until foot is desired length. The chart shows how the toe is shaped on every round. If you follow the chart, it is about 1⅜ in / 3.5 cm from the first round of decreases to the tip of the toe. If you decrease on every other round, the shaping will be narrower, with about 2¾ in / 7 cm between the first decrease round and the tip of the toe.

⑭ After completing toe shaping, cut yarn and draw end through rem sts; tighten. Weave in all ends neatly on WS.

Make the second sock the same way.

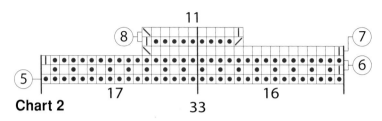

Chart 2

64

66

72
68

Chart 1

		Knit
•		Purl
☑	◩	Increase 1 with M1
◪	◪	Right-leaning decrease
◩	◪	Left-leaning decrease
⊞		Sl 1

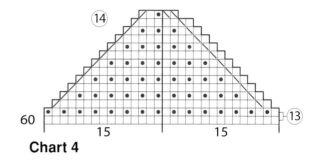

Chart 4

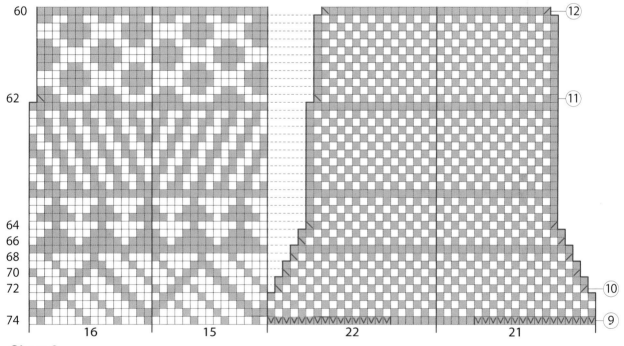

Chart 3

COWS

MATERIALS

Yarn: CYCA #1 (sock/fingering/baby) Garnstudio Drops Fabel (75% wool, 25% nylon; 224 yd/ 205 m / 50 g): one ball each Light Green, Green, and Black + a small amount of light pink for the cows' muzzles and ears and dark pink for the flowers

Needles: U.S. sizes 1.5 and 2.5 / 2.5 and 3 mm: sets of 5 dpn

Gauge: 27 sts = 4 in / 10 cm

Foot Length: You can adjust the foot length when you get to toe shaping.

These socks can be worked in several adult sizes (see the table at the beginning of this chapter).

You don't have to be a farmer to like cows! These sweet cow socks can be knitted for someone who lives in town but dreams about the good life in the countryside, where the air is fresh and the grass is green.

Instructions:

NOTE: You'll need two sizes of double-pointed needles for these socks. Use the larger dpn for the sections with two-color stranded knitting and the smaller needles for the sections with only a single color.

① With smaller dpn and White, CO 68 sts and divide sts evenly onto 4 dpn; join. The rounds begin at the side of the sock. Work following Chart 1, repeating the pattern around. Repeat the first chart row with k1, p1 ribbing for 12 rounds.

② Increase 4 sts evenly spaced around = 1 st increased on each dpn = 72 sts.

③ Repeat chart rows marked with encircled 3 6 times for a total of 13 rnds with Green.

4) On chart row marked with encircled 4, decrease 2 sts evenly spaced around = 70 sts. Change to larger dpn.

5) On chart row marked with encircled 5, decrease 2 sts evenly spaced around = 68 sts rem.

6) Repeat the two chart rows indicated by the encircled 6 six times for a total of 13 Green rnds.

⑦ Decrease 2 sts evenly spaced around = 66 sts rem.

⑧ Decrease 4 sts evenly spaced around = 62 sts rem.

⑨ Now work from Chart 2 for the heel: Cut yarn, turn work and begin 16 sts before the beginning of the round; purl 31. Place the 31 rem sts on a holder for the instep (you'll come back to these sts when the heel is finished).

⑩ Repeat these 2 rows at the encircled 10 until you've worked back and forth in stockinette for a total of 23 rows (ending with a WS row).

⑪ **Decrease:** Sl 1, k19, ssk; turn.

⑫ Repeat the following two rows until 11 sts rem (ending with a WS row):
WS: Sl 1, p9, p2tog; turn.
RS: Sl 1, k9, ssk; turn.

⑬ Now work following Chart 3 for the foot. Pick up and knit 14 sts along left side of heel flap, k11 of heel; pick up and knit 14 sts along opposite side of heel flap, and then work the 31 held sts of instep. Continue working in the round.

⑭ Decrease 1 st at each side on every third round as shown on the chart.

⑮ Now work following Chart 4 for the right sock or Chart 5 for the left sock.

⑯ Now work following Chart 6 for the toe shaping. The chart is repeated two times around. Repeat the first 2 rounds until foot is desired length. The chart shows how the toe is shaped on every round. If you follow the chart, it is about 1½ in / 3.5 cm from the first round of decreases to the tip of the toe. If you decrease on every other round, the shaping will be narrower, with about 2¾ in / 7 cm between the first decrease round and the tip of the toe.

⑰ Join the sets of sole and instep sts with Kitchener st. Weave in all ends neatly on WS.

Make the second sock the same way, mirror-imaging the cow.

⑱ Use duplicate stitch to embroider the cows' muzzles and ears and the flowers (see page 66).

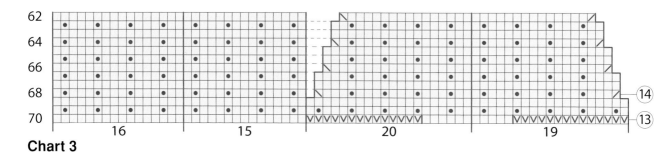

Chart 3

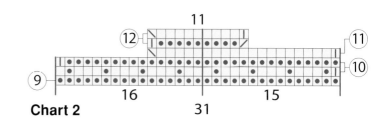

Chart 2

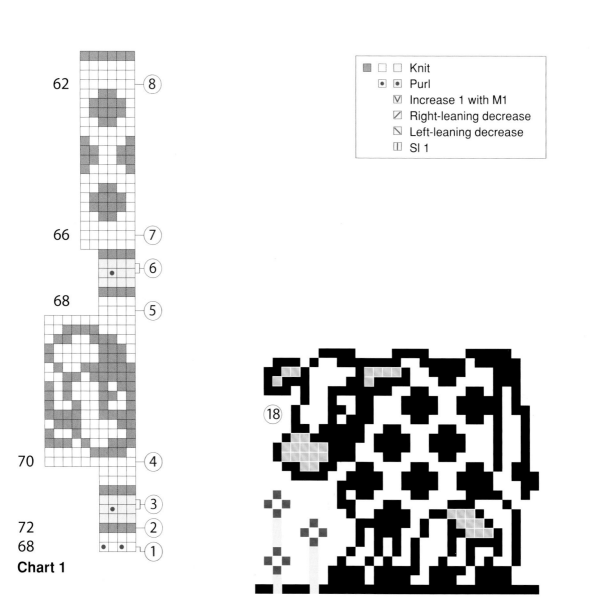

Chart 1

			Knit
•	•		Purl
	Ⅴ		Increase 1 with M1
	⧄		Right-leaning decrease
	⧅		Left-leaning decrease
	Ⅱ		Sl 1

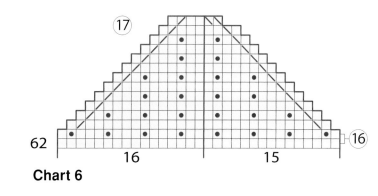

Chart 6

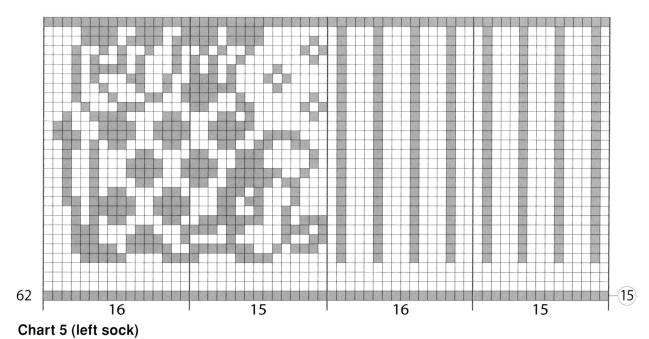

Chart 5 (left sock)

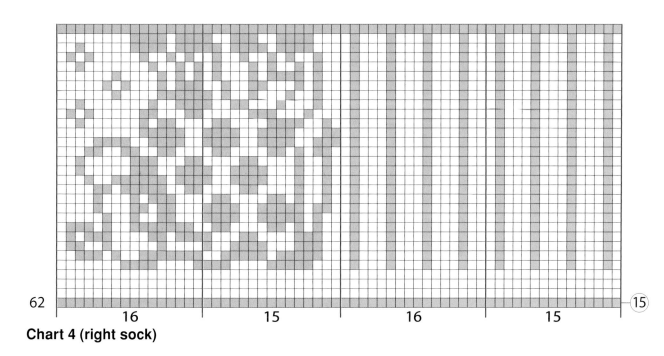

Chart 4 (right sock)

ELVES

MATERIALS

Yarn: CYCA #1 (sock/fingering/
baby) Sandnes Garn Sisu (80% wool,
20% nylon; 191 yd/ 175 m / 50 g):
one ball each White, Green, and Red
+ a small amount of black or dark
brown for the elves' eyes and boots
Needles: U.S. sizes 1.5 and 2.5 / 2.5
and 3 mm: sets of 5 dpn
Gauge: 27 sts in two-color stranded
knitting = 4 in / 10 cm

Foot Length: You can adjust the foot length
just before the toe shaping. These socks can
be worked in several adult sizes (see the table at the beginning of this chapter).

The Christmas holidays are in full swing
and the elves are dancing in a ring! The
reindeer have been set loose and are run-
ning at full speed over the countryside.
These long, fine Christmas socks make a
good Christmas gift, of course, or can be a
knitting project for the holidays.

Instructions:

NOTE: You'll need two sizes of double-pointed needles for these socks. Use the larger dpn for the sections with two-color stranded knitting and the smaller needles for the sections with only a single color.

① With smaller dpn and White, CO 68 sts and divide sts evenly onto 4 dpn; join. The rounds begin at center back of the sock. Work following Chart 1, repeating the pattern around. Change to larger dpn when the two-color pattern begins.

② At the encircled 2, increase 4 sts evenly spaced around = 1 st increased on each dpn = 72 sts.

③ At the encircled 3, decrease 4 sts evenly spaced around = 1 st decreased on each dpn = 68 sts rem.

④ At the encircled 4, decrease 4 sts evenly spaced around = 1 st decreased on each dpn = 64 sts rem.

⑤ On chart row marked with encircled 5, increase 2 sts evenly spaced around = 66 sts rem.

⑥ At the encircled 6, de-crease 2 sts evenly spaced around = 64 sts rem.

⑦ Now work from Chart 2 for the heel: cut yarn; turn work and begin 17 sts before the beginning of the rnd. P33. Place the 31 rem sts on a holder for the instep (you'll come back to these sts when the heel is finished).

⑧ Working back and forth, repeat the two rows marked by the encircled 8 for a total of 25 heel flap rows (ending with a WS row).

⑨ **Decrease:** Sl 1, k20, ssk; turn.

⑩ Repeat the 2 rows at the encircled 10 until 11 sts remain (ending with a WS row):
WS: Sl 1, p9, p2tog; turn.
RS: Sl 1, k9, ssk; turn.

⑪ Now work following Chart 3 for the foot. Pick up and knit 14 sts along left side of heel flap, k11 of heel; pick up and knit 14 sts along opposite side of heel flap, and then work the 31 held sts of instep. Continue working in the round.

⑫ Decrease 1 st at each side on every third round as shown on the chart.

⑬ Work following Chart 4 for the left sock. For the right sock, work the green/white rows on Chart 4 and then continue with the reindeer on Chart 5.

⑭ Now work following Chart 6 for the toe shaping. The chart is repeated two times around. Repeat the first 2 rounds until foot is desired length. The chart shows how the toe is shaped on every round. If you follow the chart, it is about 1½ in / 3.5 cm from the first round of decreases to the tip of the toe. If you decrease on every other round, the shaping will be narrower, with about 2¾ in / 7 cm between the first decrease round and the tip of the toe.

⑮ Join the sets of sole and instep sts with Kitchener st. Weave in all ends neatly on WS.

Make the second sock the same way, mirror-imaging the reindeer.

⑯ Use duplicate stitch to embroider the elves' eyes and boots (see page 70).

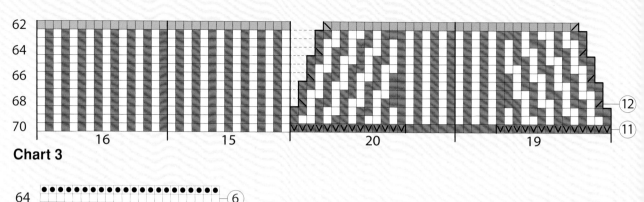

Chart 3

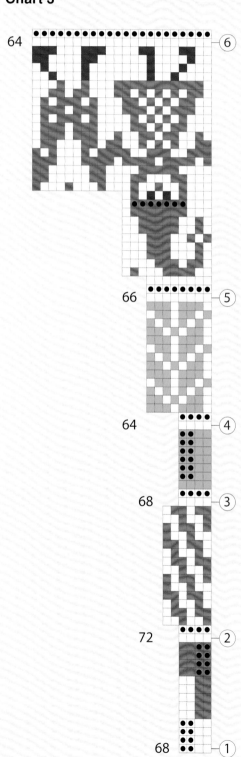

Chart 1

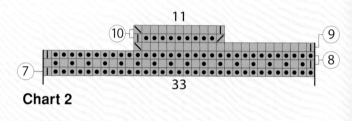

Chart 2

	Knit
•	Purl
	Increase 1 with M1
	Right-leaning decrease
	Left-leaning decrease
	Sl 1

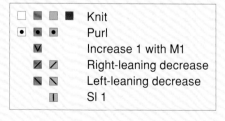

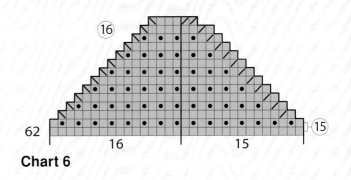

Chart 6

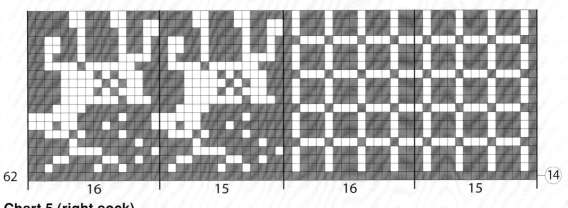
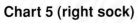

Chart 5 (right sock)

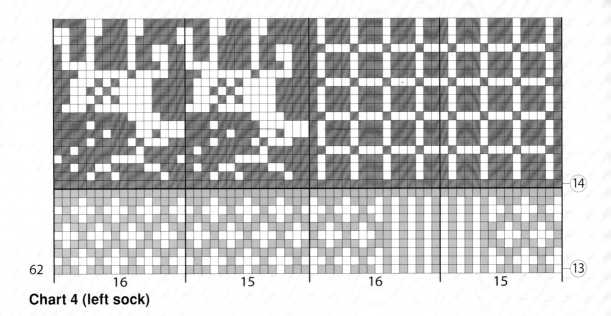

Chart 4 (left sock)

STAG FEET

MATERIALS

Yarn: CYCA #2 (sport/baby) Trysil Garn Ida (80% wool, 20% nylon; 164 yd/ 150 m / 50 g): 1 ball each Yellow Ochre, Brown, and Rust Red

Needles: U.S. sizes 1.5 and 2.5 / 2.5 and 3 mm: sets of 5 dpn

Gauge: 27 sts in two-color stranded knitting = 4 in / 10 cm

Foot Length: You can adjust the foot length just before the toe shaping. These socks can be worked in several adult sizes (see the table at the beginning of this chapter).

The stag is an animal that often appears in knitting designs. The pattern on the legs and sole indicates that it's in the forest. Perhaps these socks could be knitted for someone who likes to walk in the woods and fields?

Instructions:

NOTE: You'll need two sizes of double-pointed needles for these socks. Use the larger dpn for the sections with two-color stranded knitting and the smaller needles for the sections with only a single color.

① With smaller dpn and Brown, CO 68 sts and divide sts evenly onto 4 dpn; join. The rounds begin at center back of the sock. Work following Chart 1, repeating the pattern around. Work a total of 11 k1, p1 ribbing rounds. Change to larger dpn when the two-color pattern begins.

② At the encircled 2, increase 4 sts evenly spaced around = 1 st increased on each dpn = 72 sts.

③ At the encircled 3, decrease 4 sts evenly spaced around = 1 st decreased on each dpn = 68 sts rem.

④ Repeat the round at the encircled 4 11 times.

⑤ On chart row marked with encircled 5, decrease 4 sts evenly spaced around = 64 sts rem.

⑥ Repeat the round at the encircled 6 11 times.

⑦ Now work from Chart 2 for the heel: cut yarn; turn work and begin 17 sts before the beginning of the rnd. P33. Place the 31 rem sts on a holder for the instep (you'll come back to these sts when the heel is finished).

⑧ Working back and forth, repeat the two rows marked by the encircled 8 for a total of 25 heel flap rows (ending with a WS row).

⑨ **Decrease:** Sl 1, k20, ssk; turn.

⑩ Repeat the 2 rows at the encircled 10 until 11 sts remain (ending with a WS row):
WS: Sl 1, p9, p2tog; turn.
RS: Sl 1, k9, ssk; turn.

⑪ Now work following Chart 3 for the foot.

Pick up and knit 16 sts along left side of heel flap, k11 of heel; pick up and knit 16 sts along opposite side of heel flap, and then work the 31 held sts of instep. Continue working in the round.

⑫ Decrease 1 st at each side on every other round as shown on the chart.

⑬ Work following Chart 4.

⑭ Now check the sizing of the sock by trying it on (leave the needles in). The last 4 rows of the chart can be repeated until sock is desired length. It will be about 2 in / 5 cm from the first to last toe decrease rounds.

⑮ Continue to Chart 5, decreasing at the sides as shown on the chart.

⑯ Join the sets of sole and instep sts with Kitchener st. Weave in all ends neatly on WS.

Make the second sock the same way.

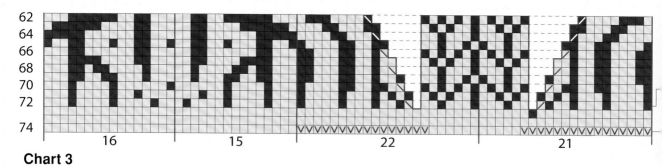

Chart 3

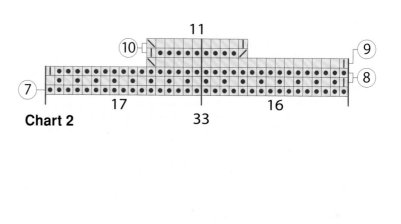

Chart 2

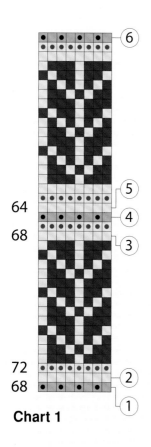

Chart 1

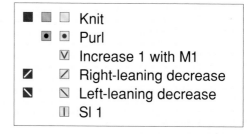

			Knit
■	▨	□	
	●	●	Purl
		Ⅴ	Increase 1 with M1
▨	◪		Right-leaning decrease
◼	◪		Left-leaning decrease
	‖		Sl 1

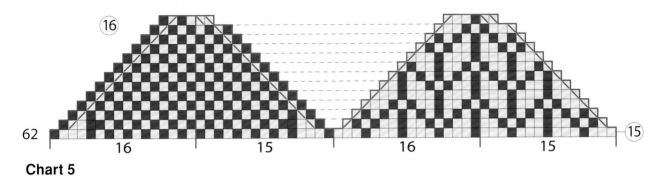

Chart 5

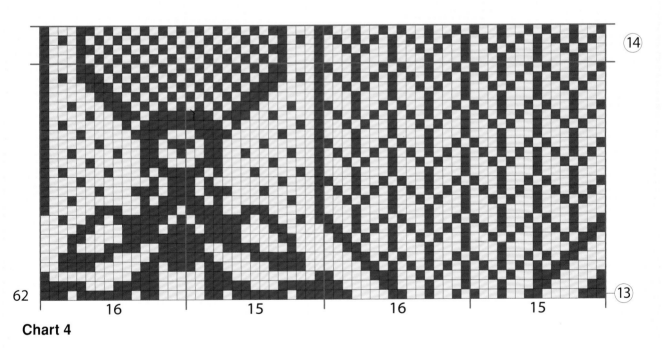

Chart 4

FLYING HEARTS

MATERIALS

Yarn: CYCA #1 (sock/fingering/baby) Viking of Norway Nordlys (75% wool, 25% nylon; 382 yd/ 349 m / 100 g): one 100 g ball each Black and multi-color #949

Needles: U.S. sizes 1.5 and 2.5 / 2.5 and 3 mm: sets of 5 dpn

Gauge: 27 sts in two-color stranded knitting = 4 in / 10 cm

Foot Length: The foot length corresponds to women's shoe size U.S. 5½- 6½ / Euro 36-37 (short) or U.S. 7½-8½ / Euro 38-39 (long). You can adjust the foot length just before the toe shaping. These socks can be worked in several adult sizes (see the table at the beginning of this chapter).

Knitters never tire of using hearts as a motif and here's a design with no shortage of them! The pattern is easy to memorize, and soon both the hearts and your needles will be flying.

Instructions:

NOTE: You'll need two sets of double-pointed needles for these socks. Use the larger dpn for the sections with two-color stranded knitting pattern and the smaller needles for the sections with only a single color.

① With smaller dpn and Black, CO 68 sts and divide sts evenly onto 4 dpn; join. The rounds begin at the side of the sock. Work following Chart 1, repeating the pattern around. Change to larger dpn when the two-color pattern begins.

② At the encircled 2, increase 4 sts evenly spaced around = 1 st increased on each dpn = 72 sts.

③ Continue by working from Chart 2.

④ Decrease 1 st at each side as shown on the chart. Repeat the round at the encircled 4 8 more times, but without any decreases.

⑤ On chart row marked with encircled 5, decrease at each side as shown on the chart. Complete Chart 2, decreasing 3 more times as indicated on chart.

⑥ Now work following Chart 3 for the heel. K31 and the place the 31 instep sts on a holder (you'll come back to these sts when the heel is finished). Do not cut yarn.

⑦ Turn work and p31 sts.

⑧ Working back and forth, repeat the two rows marked by the encircled 8 for a total of 23 heel flap rows (ending with a WS row).

⑨ **Decrease:** Sl 1, k19, ssk; turn.

⑩ Repeat the 2 rows at the encircled 10 until 11 sts remain (ending with a WS row):
WS: Sl 1, p9, p2tog; turn.
RS: Sl 1, k9, ssk; turn.

⑪ Now work following Chart 4 for the foot. Pick up and knit 16 sts

along left side of heel flap, k11 of heel; pick up and knit 16 sts along opposite side of heel flap, and then work the 31 held sts of instep. Continue working in the round.

⑫ Decrease 1 st at each side on every other round as shown on the chart until 62 sts rem.

⑬ Work following Chart 5.

⑭ Now check the sizing of the sock by trying it on (leave the needles in). It will be about 2 in / 5 cm from the first to last toe decrease rounds. If the sock is too short, continue working from Chart 6 until sock is desired length before toe shaping.

⑮ **Toe Shaping:** Decrease 2 sts at each side as shown on the chart.

⑯ Join the sets of sole and instep sts with Kitchener st. Weave in all ends neatly on WS.

Make the second sock the same way.

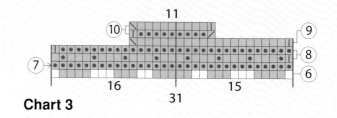

Chart 3

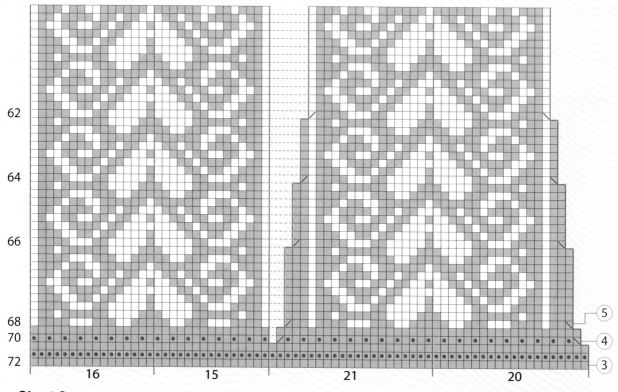

Chart 2

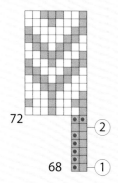

Chart 1

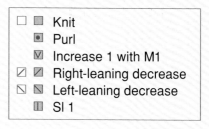

	Knit
	Purl
	Increase 1 with M1
	Right-leaning decrease
	Left-leaning decrease
	Sl 1

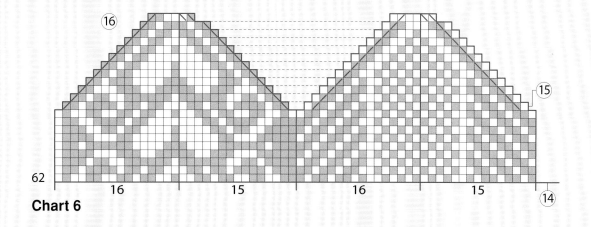

Chart 6

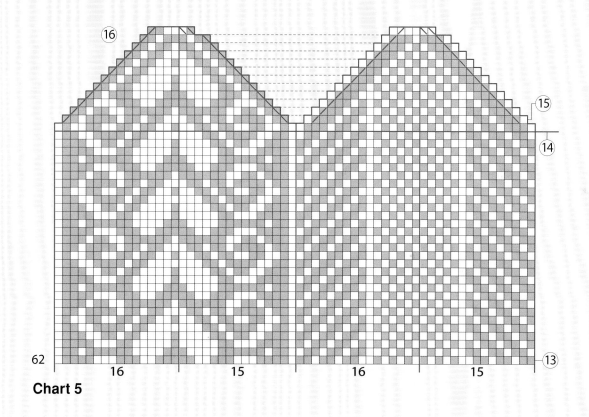

Chart 5

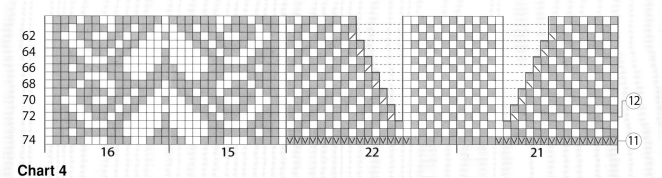

Chart 4

TALLULAH'S HEART

MATERIALS

Yarn: CYCA #1 (sock/fingering/ baby) Viking of Norway Nordlys (75% wool, 25% nylon; 382 yd/ 349 m / 100 g): one 100 g ball each White and multicolor #949

Needles: U.S. sizes 1.5 and 2.5 / 2.5 and 3 mm: sets of 5 dpn

Gauge: 27 sts in two-color stranded knitting = 4 in / 10 cm

Foot Length: The foot length corresponds to women's shoe size U.S. 5½-6½ / Euro 36-37 (short) or U.S. 7½-8½ / Euro 38-39 (long). You can adjust the foot length just before the toe shaping. These socks can be worked in several adult sizes (see the table at the beginning of this chapter).

"Tallulah" is a name which some say means "leaping water." The design of these socks was inspired by the way water can form heart-shaped swirls. Perhaps you know someone who'd be delighted to get a pair of socks with Tallulah's hearts on them? If you have a tendency to be bored by knitting socks with lots of identical rounds, this pattern is for you.

Instructions:

NOTE: You'll need two sizes of double-pointed needles for these socks. Use the larger dpn for the sections with two-color stranded knitting and the smaller needles for the sections with only a single color.

① With smaller dpn and White, CO 70 sts and divide sts evenly onto 4 dpn; join. The rounds begin at the side of the sock. Work following Chart 1, repeating the pattern around. The first 6 rounds are a little lace pattern that rolls forward. Change to larger dpn when the two-color pattern begins.

② Repeat the round at the encircled 2, with k3, p2 ribbing, 12 times.

③ At the encircled 3, increase 1 st at each side = 72 sts.

④ Decrease 2 sts at each side as shown on the chart. = 68 sts rem.

⑤ Now work from Chart 2. On the first rnd, de-crease 1 st at each side as shown and then repeat the decrease two more times where indicated on chart.

⑥ Next, begin the heel. K31.

⑦ Turn work and p31 sts. Place the 31 instep sts on a holder (you'll come back to these sts when the heel is finished). Do not cut yarn.

⑧ Working back and forth, repeat the two rows marked by the encircled 8 for a total of 25 heel flap rows (ending with a WS row).

⑨ **Decrease:** Sl 1, k19, ssk; turn.

⑩ Repeat the 2 rows at the encircled 10 until 11 sts remain (ending with a WS row):
WS: Sl 1, p9, p2tog; turn.
RS: Sl 1, k9, ssk; turn.

⑪ Now work following Chart 3 for the foot.
Rnd 1: Pick up and knit 16 sts along left side of heel flap, k11 of heel; pick up and knit 16 sts along opposite side of heel flap, and then work the 31 held sts of instep. Continue working in the round.

⑫ Decrease 1 st at each side on every other round as shown on the chart.

⑬ Work following Chart 4.

⑭ Now check the sizing of the sock by trying it on (leave the needles in). The last 4 rows of the chart can be repeated until sock is desired length. It will be about 2 in / 5 cm from the first to last toe decrease rounds. If you see that the sock will be too short, continue working to end of Chart 5 so the toe length will be 2½ in / 6 cm.

⑮ Decrease 2 sts at each side as shown on the chart.

⑯ Join the sets of sole and instep sts with Kitchener st. Weave in all ends neatly on WS.

Make the second sock the same way.

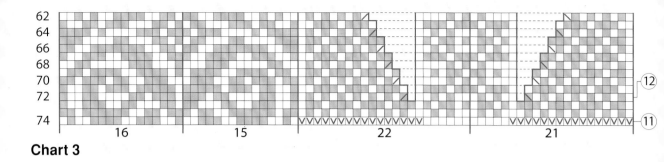

Chart 3

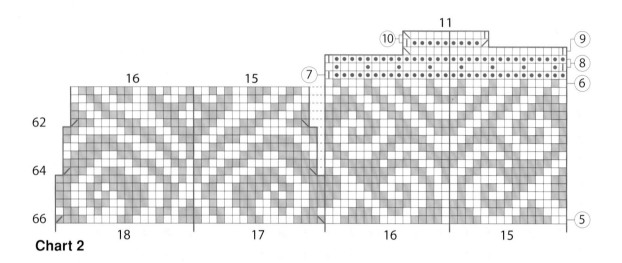

Chart 2

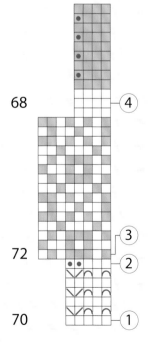

Chart 1

		Knit
⊡	⊡	Purl
⋁		Increase 1 with M1
⧄	⧄	Right-leaning decrease
⧅	⧅	Left-leaning decrease
⊓	⊓	Sl 1
⌒		Yarnover

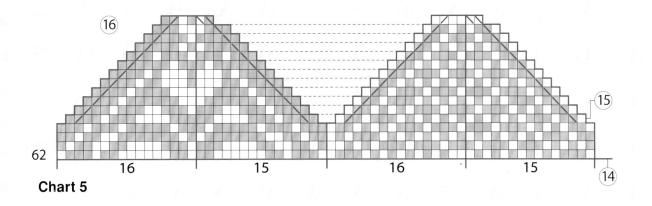

Chart 5

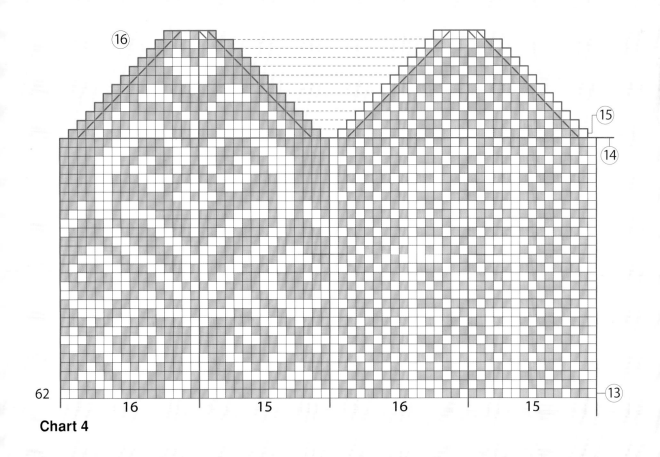

Chart 4

VIKING

MATERIALS

Yarn: CYCA #1 (sock/fingering/baby) Sandnes Garn Sisu (80% wool, 20% nylon; 191 yd/ 175 m / 50 g): 2 balls of Black and 1 ball each Dark Red and Beige

Needles: U.S. sizes 1.5 and 2.5 / 2.5 and 3 mm: sets of 5 dpn

Gauge: 27 sts in two-color stranded knitting = 4 in / 10 cm

Foot Length: You can adjust the foot length just before the toe shaping. With the recommended yarn and needles, the socks should fit women's shoe sizes U.S. 5½-9½ / Euro 36-40. These socks can be worked in several adult sizes (see the table at the beginning of this chapter).

The patterning in these socks was inspired by intricate Viking cables that decorated houses, jewelry, and boats. The result is a pair of formidable socks that will suit both women and men.

Instructions:

NOTE: You'll need two sizes of double-pointed needles for these socks. Use the larger dpn for the sections with two-color stranded knitting and the smaller needles for the sections with only a single color.

① With smaller dpn and Black, CO 68 sts and divide sts evenly onto 4 dpn; join. The rounds begin at center back of the sock. Work following Chart 1, repeating the pattern around. Change to larger dpn when the two-color pattern begins.

② At the encircled 2, increase 4 sts (M1 before the first st on each dpn) evenly spaced around = 72 sts.

③ At the encircled 3, decrease 4 sts (k2tog at beginning of each needle) evenly spaced around = 1 st decreased on each dpn = 68 sts rem.

④ Now work from Chart 2.

⑤ On chart row marked with encircled 5, decrease 2 sts at center back as shown on the chart = 66 sts rem. Decrease once more where indicated = 64 sts rem.

⑥ **Heel:** K17 on the next rnd.

⑦ Now work from Chart 3 for the heel: turn work and p33. Place the 31 rem sts on a holder for the instep (you'll come back to these sts when the heel is finished).

⑧ Working back and forth with Black, repeat the two rows marked by the encircled 8 for a total of 25 heel flap rows (ending with a WS row).

⑨ **Decrease:** Sl 1, k20, ssk; turn.

⑩ Repeat the 2 rows at the encircled 10 until 11 sts remain (ending with a WS row):
WS: Sl 1, p9, p2tog; turn.
RS: Sl 1, k9, ssk; turn.

⑪ Now work following Chart 4 for the foot. Pick up and knit 16 sts along left side of heel flap, k11 of heel; pick up and knit 16 sts along opposite side of heel flap, and then work the 31 held sts of instep. Continue working in the round.

⑫ Decrease 1 st at each side on every other round as shown on the chart.

⑬ Repeat the 8 rows at the encircled 13 until the foot is desired length before toe shaping.

⑭ Now work following Chart 5 for the toe shaping. The chart is repeated two times around. The chart shows how the toe is shaped on every round. If you follow the chart, it is about 1½ in / 3.5 cm from the first round of decreases to the tip of the toe. If you decrease on every other round, the shaping will be narrower, with about 2¾ in / 7 cm between the first decrease round and the tip of the toe.

⑮ Join the sets of sole and instep sts with Kitchener st. Weave in all ends neatly on WS.

Make the second sock the same way.

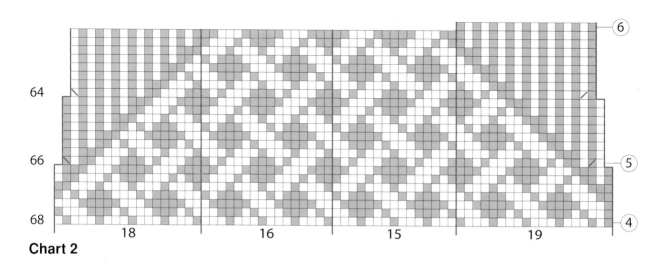

64
66
68
18 16 15 19

Chart 2

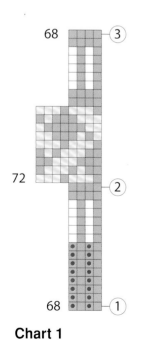

68 ③
72 ②
68 ①

Chart 1

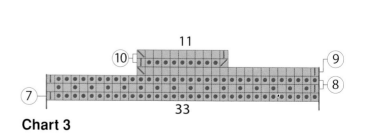

11
10 ⑨
7 ⑧
33

Chart 3

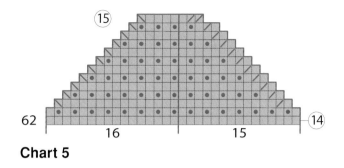

Chart 5

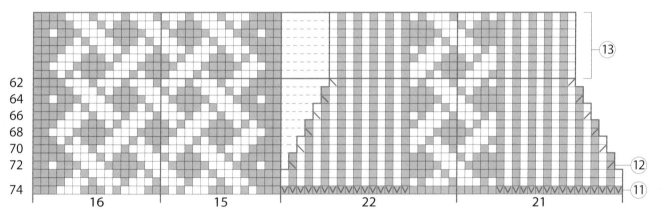

Chart 4

		Knit
☐ ☐ ■		
⊡	⊡	Purl
	Ⅴ	Increase 1 with M1
⧄	⧄	Right-leaning decrease
⧅	⧅	Left-leaning decrease
	▥	Sl 1

MOTHER-IN-LAW'S
SOCKS

My mother-in-law knits all the time. Everyone in her social circle could expect lovely, thick socks as a gift because she always had her sock knitting (sokkebinding in the local dialect) in her hands. Relatives and friends were sure to have warm feet even on ice-cold days, because my mother-in-law always used thick, high-quality wool yarn for the socks she knitted.

Her children and grandchildren actually had so many pairs of socks that we still have some in reserve, even several years after she died. It was an inheritance we are very grateful for.

Her socks have a somewhat different heel shaping than the one my mother taught me. The heel is worked back and forth and shaped with a few decreases at the center of the heel turn—a simple concept that is very conducive to knitting the heel with two-color stripes.

This type of heel shaping is ideal for anyone who wears extra socks in boots. Even if the sock skews in the boot, there won't be any wear holes along the shaping line under the heel—quite simply because there is no decrease line there.

MOTHER-IN-LAW'S
SOCKS

These socks are knitted with a wool yarn worked at a gauge of 24 sts in 4 in / 10 cm. A good yarn choice is Sterk (CYCA #3, DK) from Du Store Alpakka, knitted on U.S. 2.5 / 3 mm needles (set of 5 dpn). The basic pattern can be used for all sizes.

Here you can see a pair of my mother-in-law's hand knitted socks that we saved. They're tried and true, practical socks that were knitted with love and with thoughts of warmth and comfort for the recipient.

Basic Pattern for Mother-in-Law's Socks:

SIZES: Men's (Women's, Children's)

CO 56 (48, 44). Divide sts evenly onto 4 dpn and join to work in the round.

Beginning with k2, work around in k2, p2 ribbing for 70 (64, 54) rounds.

Heel: Work back and forth in stockinette over half the total sts in the round. The rem sts are set aside for the instep while you work the heel.

NOTE: For Men's and Women's sizes, begin the round 1 st before the beginning of the round, so that the edge of the heel will align symmetrically over the knit and purl sts in the ribbing.

Work in stockinette over the next 28 (24, 22) sts and, *at the same time*, on the first row, increase 4 sts evenly spaced across to 32 (28, 26) sts. Work back and forth for 18 (16, 14) rows.

Heel Shaping: The heel is shaped by decreasing on every other row (= on RS rows) 3 times at the center back of the heel. This produces a nicely rounded heel. Divide the heel sts over 2 needles = 16 (14, 13) sts on each dpn.
RS rows: Knit until 3 sts rem on the first needle, k2tog, k1. Needle 2: K1, ssk (or k2tog tbl), knit to end of row.
WS rows: Purl.
After completing the 3 decrease rows [= 26 (22, 20) sts rem], on the next RS row, knit until 2 sts rem on needle 1, k2tog; begin needle 2 with ssk and knit to end of row.
Now seam the underside of the heel with Kitchener st: fold the heel at the center, making sure you have the same number of sts on each of the two needles. Cut yarn, leaving a tail long enough to graft the sts. Join the sets of sts with Kitchener st and fasten off.

Foot: Begin at the top of the left side edge of the heel.
Needles 1 and 2: Pick up and knit 16 (14, 13) sts along each side edge.
Needles 3 and 4: Work the 28 (24, 22) instep sts. The instep continues in k2, p2 ribbing to the end of the sock, while the sole is worked in stockinette.

Try on the sock or check the sizing table at the beginning of the book and continue as est until the foot is desired length before toe shaping. The toe will be about 2¼ (1½, 1¼) in / 5.5 (4, 3.5) cm from the first decrease to the tip of the toe. Shape toe by decreasing on each side of the foot: Ssk or k2tog tbl, work until 2 sts rem on instep/sole, k2tog). Knit the next round.

Continue decreasing at each side on every other round. When 6 or 8 sts remain, join the sets of sole and instep sts with Kitchener st.

MOTHER-IN-LAW'S SOCKS FOR LITTLE FEET

A deer fawn or Maria ladybug? Why not let the child decide? Since these socks are small, they take almost no time to knit, so perhaps a pair of each.

These socks will be the same size because they're knitted with the same type of yarn and the same needles.

You'll need one ball of each color to knit a pair.

FOOT LENGTH	SHOE SIZE	YARN	NEEDLES	GAUGE IN 4 IN / 10 CM
U.S. 4¼-5¼ in	4½-7	Baby yarn	1.5	28-30 sts
Euro 11-13.5 cm	20-23		2.5 mm	
U.S. 5½-6¾ in	8-11½	Fine Sock	1.5-2.5	26-27 sts
Euro 14-17 cm	24-29		2.5-3 mm	
U.S. 7-7½ in	12½-1	Heavy Sock	1.5-2.5	24-25 sts
Euro 18-19 cm	30-32		2.5-3 mm	
U.S. 8-8½ in	2-4½	Heavy Sock	2.5-4	22-23 sts
Euro 20-21.5 cm	33-35		3-3.5 mm	

LITTLE
DEER FAWN

MATERIALS

Yarn: CYCA #1 (sock/fingering/baby) Dale Babyull (100% Merino wool; 180 yd/165 m / 50 g): 1 ball each White and Dark Beige

Needles: U.S. size 2.5 / 3 mm: set of 5 dpn

Foot Length: 6-6¾ in / 15-17 cm. The heel and toe are reinforced with alternating slip stitches to tighten the knitting. The socks can be adjusted to fit all children's sizes (see the table at the beginning of this chapter).

The fawn, with its best friend, a little bird sitting on its back, is out and about in the pretty winter landscape. Surrounding the sock leg are trees where the young fawn and its friend can play hide-and-seek.

Instructions:

① With White, CO 48 sts and divide sts evenly onto 4 dpn; join. The rounds begin at the side of the sock. Work following Chart 1, repeating the pattern around.

② At the encircled 2, increase 2 sts evenly spaced around = 50 sts.

③ At the encircled 3, work the last round before the heel: Increase 1 st with M1, k13, M1, k13, M1, knit to end of rnd = 53 sts.

④ Continue by working Chart 2 for the heel flap: The heel is worked back and forth over the first 27 sts of the round. Place the 26 rem sts on a holder for the instep (you'll come back to these sts when the heel is finished). Slip sts as shown on the chart for a tighter fabric and to produce a stable edge on the sides.

⑤ Decrease at the center of the heel on every 4th row as shown on the chart.

⑥ On the last row of the heel, decrease 3 times at the center. Fold the heel in half and join the 9 sts on each side with dark yarn and Kitchener st.

⑦ Continue, following Chart 3, for the foot: **Rnd 1:** Pick up and knit 13 sts along each side of the heel (2 sts in each stripe). Knit the 26 held sts for instep.

⑧ **Toe Shaping:** With Dark yarn only, knit until foot is desired length before toe shaping. The chart shows how the toe is shaped. If you follow the chart, it is about 1¼ in / 3 cm from the first round of decreases to the tip of the toe. **NOTE:** Some of the toe rounds have slip stitches to reinforce the knitting— see chart.

⑨ Cut yarn, leaving a tail long enough to join the sets of sole and instep sts with Kitchener st. Weave in all ends neatly on WS.

Make the second sock the same way, using Chart 4 for the foot so the calf turns the opposite direction.

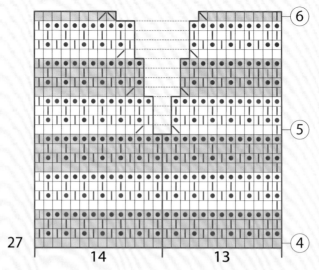

Chart 2

27

14 13

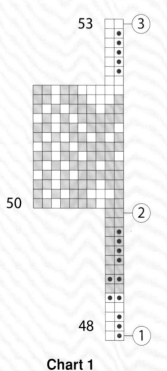

53 ③

50 ②

48 ①

Chart 1

		Knit
		Purl
		Increase 1 with M1
		Right-leaning decrease
		Left-leaning decrease
		Sl 1

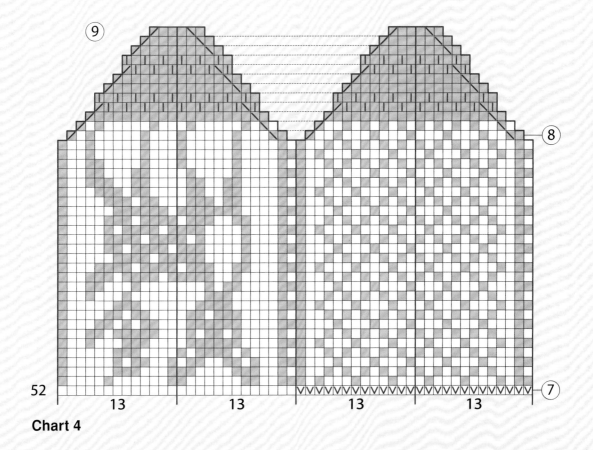

Chart 4

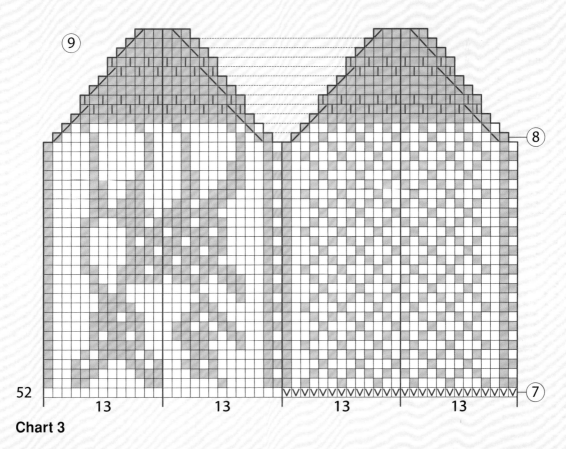

Chart 3

MARIA LADYBUG

MATERIALS

Yarn: CYCA #1 (sock/fingering/baby)
Rauma Baby Panda (100% Merino wool;
191 yd/175 m / 50 g): 1 ball each Black,
Green, White and Red (enough for several
pairs)

Needles: U.S. sizes 1.5 and 2.5 / 2.5 and 3
mm: sets of 5 dpn

Foot Length: 4¾-6 in / 12-15 cm. After the
knitting is complete, you can embroider on
the eyes, snout, and antennae.

Most of each sock is worked with a
single strand of yarn so you might want
to use the smaller needles for those
sections. Use the larger needles for the
two-color stranded knitting.

It's said to be lucky to have a ladybug
land on your hand. Good luck is guaranteed in any case for anyone who
receives these fine little socks with a
ladybug on each foot.

Instructions:

① With Green and smaller dpn, CO 48 sts and divide sts evenly onto 4 dpn; join. The rounds begin at the side of the sock. Work following Chart 1, repeating the pattern around. Don't forget to change to larger dpn for the two-color pattern rows and then back to smaller for the stripes.

② Continue to Chart 2 for the heel. K12 on the next rnd.

③ Turn the work and p24. Place the rem 24 sts on a holder for the instep (you'll come back to these sts when the heel is finished). Continue in stockinette, working back and forth with 9 rows for the heel flap

④ On the row with the encircled 4, decrease 2 sts at center back on every other row as shown on the chart.

⑤ On the last row of the heel, k5, decrease 2 times at the center (see chart). Cut yarn, leaving a long tail for grafting. Fold the heel in half and join the sts on each side Kitchener st.

⑥ Continue, following Chart 3, for the foot:
Rnd 1: Pick up and knit 12 sts along each side of the heel. Knit the 24 held sts for instep = 48 sts.

⑦ At the encircled 7, increase 4 sts as shown on the chart = 52 sts total. Change to larger dpn.

⑧ Begin the toe shaping at the encircled 8. Follow the chart until 12 sts rem.

⑨ Cut yarn, leaving a tail long enough to join the sets of sole and instep sts with Kitchener st. Weave in all ends neatly on WS.

⑩ Using duplicate stitch and beginning with white for the eyes, embroider the eyes and head on the ladybug. To embroider the antennae, work long stitches on each side of the head.

Make the second sock the same way.

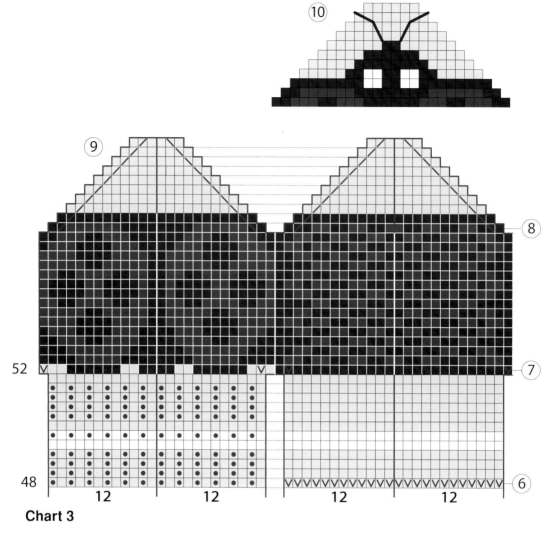

⑩

⑨

52

48

Chart 3

12 12 12 12

⑧

⑦

⑥

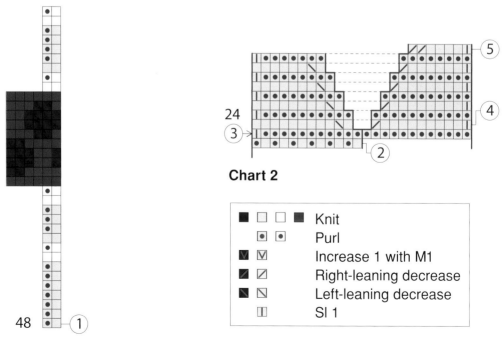

⑤

④

③

②

24

Chart 2

				Knit
				Purl
				Increase 1 with M1
				Right-leaning decrease
				Left-leaning decrease
				Sl 1

48

①

Chart 1

MOTHER-IN-LAW'S SOCKS
FOR BIGGER FEET

These socks have nothing to decrease except for the fine and easy heel shaping because these socks have a completely different look. Knit a pair that best matches the interests of the person who will get the socks.

The socks can be knitted in a variety of sizes. Choose yarn and needles that will combine to give you the gauge for the right size.

FOOT LENGTH	SHOE SIZE	YARN	NEEDLES	GAUGE IN 4 IN / 10 CM
U.S. 8¾-9 in **Euro** 22-23 cm	5½-6½ 36-37	Fine Sock	1.5 2.5 mm	28-30 sts
U.S. 9½-9¾ in **Euro** 24-25 cm	7½ -9½ 38-40	Fine Sock	1.5-2.5 2.5-3 mm	26-27 sts
U.S. 10¼-10¾ in **Euro** 26-27 cm	10½-10* 41-43	Heavy Sock	2.5-4 3-3.5 mm	24-25 sts
U.S. 11-11 ¾ in **Euro** 28-30 cm	10*-13* 44-46	Heavy Sock	4-6 3.5-4 mm	22-23 sts

Men's size; all other sizes are women's

THE KNITTING CLUB'S
FAVORITE—
FOR ADULTS

MATERIALS

Yarn: CYCA #2 (sport/baby) Dale Garn Falk (100% wool; 116 yd/106 m / 50 g): 1 ball each Yellow, Orange, Red, and White

Needles: U.S. size 2.5 / 3 mm: set of 5 dpn

If you use relatively heavy yarn and have many stitches around, the socks will fit well on the feet. The alterations between the color pattern knitting and the ribbing make the knitting elastic, so these socks will fit many sizes. You can

adjust the foot length when you get to the toe shaping.

These socks have earned their name, "favorite," for several reasons: They're easy to knit, you can choose among many colors, and they're so comfortable to wear.

As a starting point, the socks use the same pattern as for the child's size described earlier in the book, but the adult sizes have several colors and use my mother-in-law's heel shaping.

Instructions:

① With Yellow, CO 60 sts and divide sts evenly onto 4 dpn; join. The rounds begin at the side of the sock. Work following Chart 1, repeating the pattern around. The first round is repeated 8 times so that a rolled edge forms.

② After completing Chart 1, continue by working Chart 2 for the heel flap: beginning with the first 31 sts of the round, work back and forth. Place the 29 rem sts on a holder for the instep (you'll come back to these sts when the heel is finished).

③ At the encircled 3, decrease 2 sts at the back of the heel on every other round as shown on the chart.

④ On the last heel row, decrease 3 sts (see chart)

so you'll have the same stitch count on each side. Cut yarn, leaving a long enough tail for grafting. Fold the heel in half and join the two sets of sts with Kitchener st.

⑤ Now work following Chart 3 for the foot. **Rnd 1:** Pick up and knit 15 sts along left side of heel and then pick up and knit 16 sts on other side of heel. Continue over the 29 sts of the instep. Place markers on each side of the sole so you'll remember not to purl any sts in the pattern on the sole.

⑥ Now work the foot following the pattern for the instep as before on the leg; work the pattern on the foot but without any purl sts. Continue as est until foot is desired length to toe shaping.

⑦ **Toe Shaping:** Work from Chart 4. Repeat the charted sts two times around. If you follow the chart, the toe will be 2 in / 5 cm from the start of the decreasing to the tip of the toe. If you decrease on every other round, the shaping will be narrower, with about 3½ in / 9 cm between the first decrease round and the tip of the toe. Work in est pattern from beginning of toe shaping using only one color and purl sts only on the instep.

⑧ Cut yarn and draw end through rem sts; tighten. Weave in all ends neatly on WS.

Make the second sock the same way.

Legend

☐	▨	◼	☐	Knit
⊡	⊡	⊡	⊡	Purl
		☑		Increase 1 with M1
	▧	◿		Right-leaning decrease
	◼	◥		Left-leaning decrease
▥	▥	▥		Sl 1

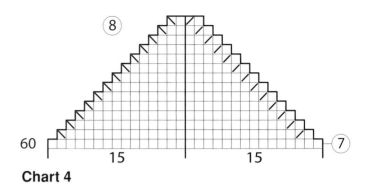

Chart 4

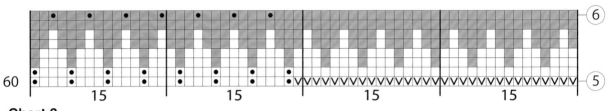

Chart 3

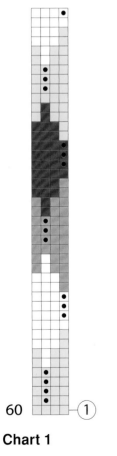

Chart 1

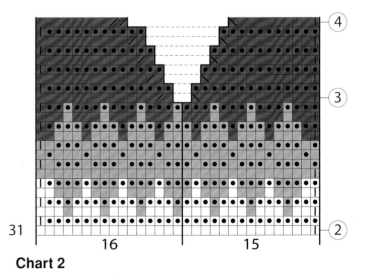

Chart 2

JORID'S CHRISTMAS HEARTS

MATERIALS

Yarn: CYCA #1 (sock/fingering/baby) Sandnes Garn Sisu (80% wool, 20% nylon; 191 yd/ 175 m / 50 g): one ball each Red, Blue, and White

Needles: U.S. size 2.5 / 3 mm: set of 5 dpn

Socks with red hearts just scream Christmas and are the perfect Christmas gift. The legs feature a typical winter landscape with snow-covered spruces against a dark blue winter night sky.

Instructions:

① With White, CO 60 sts and divide sts evenly onto 4 dpn; join. The rounds begin at the side of the sock. Work following Chart 1, repeating the pattern around.

② Continue by working Chart 2 for the heel flap: beginning with the first 31 sts of the round, work back and forth. Place the 29 rem sts on a holder for the instep (you'll come back to these sts when the heel is finished).

③ Repeat the four rows at the encircled 3 three times for a total of 4 white stripes on the heel.

④ Decrease 2 sts at center back of the heel on every other row as shown on the chart.

⑤ On the last heel row, work 7 sts and then decrease 3 times as shown on the chart. Cut yarn, leaving a long enough tail of Red for grafting. Fold the heel in half and join the two sets of sts with Kitchener st, matching the colors on each side.

⑥ Now work following Chart 3 for the foot.
Rnd 1: Pick up and knit 15 sts along each side of heel, increase 1 st before the instep, and work the 29 instep sts.

⑦ Repeat the 4 rows at the encircled 7 4 times.

⑧ Continue in stripe pattern until foot is desired length to beginning of toe shaping. If you follow the chart, the toe will be 2 in / 5 cm from the start of the decreasing to the tip of the toe. If you decrease on every other round, the shaping will be narrower, with about 3½ in / 9 cm between the first decrease round and the tip of the toe.

⑨ Cut yarn and draw end through rem sts; tighten. Weave in all ends neatly on WS.

Make the second sock the same way.

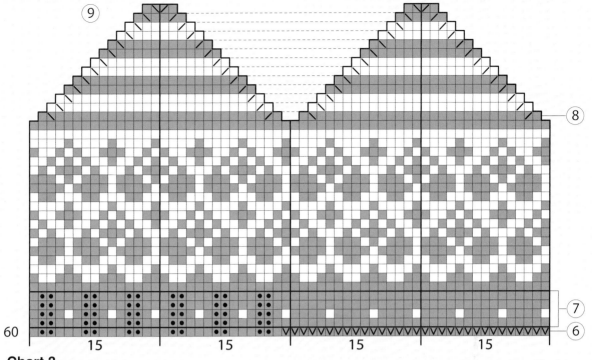

⑨

⑧

⑦

⑥

60

15   15   15   15

Chart 3

		■	Knit
●	·		Purl
Ⅴ			Increase 1 with M1
◩	⬧		Right-leaning decrease
◩	◺		Left-leaning decrease
❙	❙		Sl 1

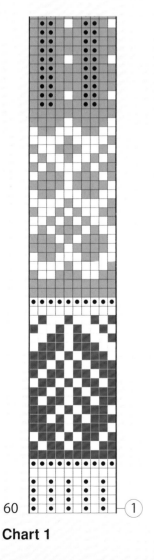

60   ①

Chart 1

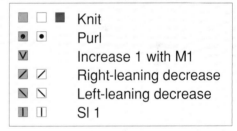

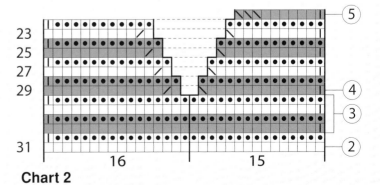

⑤

23
25
27
29   ④
          ③
31   ②

16   15

Chart 2

NORDIC SOCKS

MATERIALS

Yarn: CYCA #1 (sock/fingering/baby) Sandnes Garn Sisu (80% wool, 20% nylon; 191 yd/ 175 m / 50 g): one ball each Light Beige Heather #3021, Red #4228, Orange #3326, Dark Sea-green #5626, and Brown #3082
Needles: U.S. sizes 1.5 and 2.5 / 2.5 and 3 mm: sets of 5 dpn

These socks have a typical Nordic look to them. The wonderful colors spill out in layers with each other and are arranged in panels of varying widths and patterns. A total of five different colors are used. However, if you buy two balls of Light Beige Heather and use leftovers yarns for the other colors, you'll have enough yarn for a pair of the socks described on the next page.

Instructions:

NOTE: You'll need two sizes of double-pointed needles for these socks. Use the larger dpn for the sections with two-color stranded knitting and the smaller needles for the sections with only a single color.

① With Light Beige Heather and smaller dpn, CO 64 sts and divide sts evenly onto 4 dpn; join. The rounds begin at the center back of the sock. Work following Chart 1, repeating the pattern around. The first chart row of k1, p1 ribbing is repeated for 12 rounds.

② On the round with the encircled 2, increase 4 sts evenly spaced around = 68 sts.

③ At the encircled 3, decrease 3 sts evenly spaced around = 65 sts rem.

④ Decrease 1 st = 64 sts rem.

⑤ Continue by working Chart 2 for the heel: K16 sts; turn and p32. Work back and forth over the 32 heel sts until you've completed 20 rows for the heel. Place the 32 rem sts on a holder for the instep (you'll come back to these sts when the heel is finished).

⑥ Shape the heel by decreasing at center back on every other row as shown on the chart.

⑦ On the last heel row, work 5 sts and then decrease 2 times as shown on the chart. Cut yarn, leaving a long enough tail for grafting. Fold the heel in half and join the two sets of sts with Kitchener st.

⑧ Now work following Chart 3 for the foot. The round begins at the center of the sole. Beginning at the center of the heel, pick up and knit 16 sts along the right side, continue over the 32 instep sts, pick up and knit 16 sts on

left side of heel, and knit to end of rnd. Divide the sts with 16 sts on each of 4 dpn and continue in pattern.

⑨ At the encircled 9, work in stripes until foot is desired length before toe shaping. If you follow the chart, the toe will be 2 in / 5 cm from the start of the decreasing to the tip of the toe.

⑩ **Toe Shaping:** Work from Chart 3. The pattern is repeated twice so the top and bottom of the toe are the same. If necessary, repeat the chart row at encircled 10 to adjust toe length. When shaping, 2 sts are decreased at each side of the foot as shown on the chart.

⑪ Cut yarn and draw end through rem sts; tighten. Weave in all ends neatly on WS.

Make the second sock the same way.

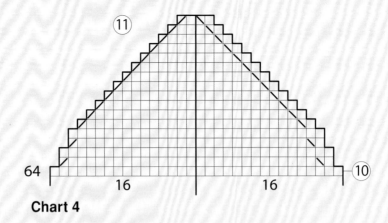

Chart 4

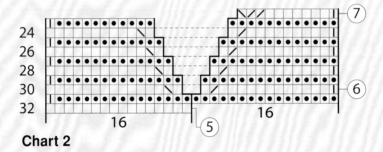

Chart 2

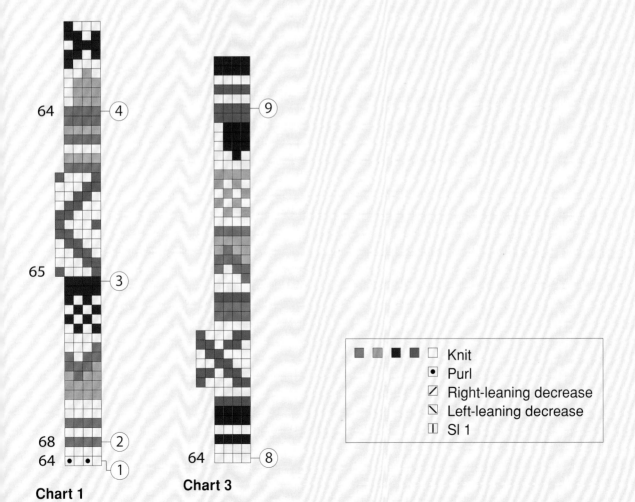

Chart 1

Chart 3

Knit
Purl
Right-leaning decrease
Left-leaning decrease
Sl 1

THE BIG LEFTOVER PARTY

If you buy an extra ball of the Light Beige Heather for the Nordic Socks, then you can use leftovers for all the other colors.

MATERIALS

Yarn: CYCA #1 (sock/fingering/baby) Sandnes Garn Sisu (80% wool, 20% nylon; 191 yd/ 175 m / 50 g): one ball Light Beige Heather #3021 and leftover amounts of Red #4228, Orange #3326, Dark Sea-green #5626, and Brown #3082

Needles: U.S. sizes 1.5 and 2.5 / 2.5 and 3 mm: sets of 5 dpn

If you bought yarn for the previous pair of socks (Nordic Socks), then you'll have enough left over for this pair. Beware—you'll have plenty of ends to weave in when finishing. The pattern panels are typical "filling patterns," arranged so that the panels have alternating diagonal and straight patterns. These socks are the same size as the Nordic socks.

Instructions:

NOTE: You'll need two sizes of double-pointed needles for these socks. Use the larger dpn for the sections with two-color stranded knitting and the smaller needles for the sections with only a single color.

① With Dark Sea-green and smaller dpn, CO 64 sts and divide sts evenly onto 4 dpn; join. The rounds begin at the center back of the sock. Work following Chart 1, repeating the pattern around. The first rnd of k1, p1 ribbing is repeated for 12 rounds.

② On the round with the encircled 2, increase 5 sts evenly spaced around = 69 sts. Don't forget to change to larger dpn when the two-color patterns begin.

③ At the encircled 3, decrease 3 sts evenly spaced around = 66 sts rem.

④ At the encircled 4, decrease 2 sts evenly spaced around = 64 sts rem.

⑤ Continue by working Chart 2 for the heel: K16

sts; turn and p32. Place the 32 rem sts on a holder for the instep (you'll come back to these sts when the heel is finished). Work back and forth over the 32 heel sts until you've completed 20 rows for the heel.

⑥ Shape the heel by decreasing at center back on every other row as shown on the chart.

⑦ On the last heel row, work 5 sts and then decrease 2 times as shown on the chart. Cut yarn, leaving a long enough tail for grafting. Fold the heel in half and join the two sets of sts with Kitchener st.

⑧ Now work following Chart 3 for the foot. The round begins at the center of the sole. Beginning at the center of the heel, pick up and knit 17 sts along the right side, continue over the 32 instep sts, and then pick up and knit 17 sts on left side of heel. Divide the sts with 16 sts on each of the instep needles and 17 each on the

sole needles; continue in pattern.

⑨ At the encircled 9, decrease 2 sts evenly spaced across the sole = 64 sts rem.

⑩ On the row marked with the encircled 10, decrease 4 sts evenly spaced around = 60 sts rem. Repeat the final motif until the foot is desired length to beginning of toe shaping. If you follow the chart, the toe will be 2 in / 5 cm from the start of the decreasing to the tip of the toe.

⑪ **Toe Shaping:** Work from Chart 3. The pattern is repeated twice so the top and bottom of the toe are the same. When shaping, 2 sts are decreased at each side of the foot as shown on the chart.

⑫ Cut yarn and draw end through rem sts; tighten. Weave in all ends neatly on WS.

Make the second sock the same way.

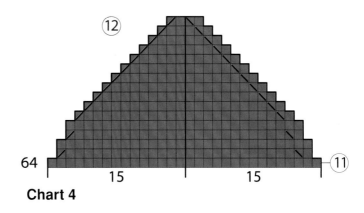

Chart 4

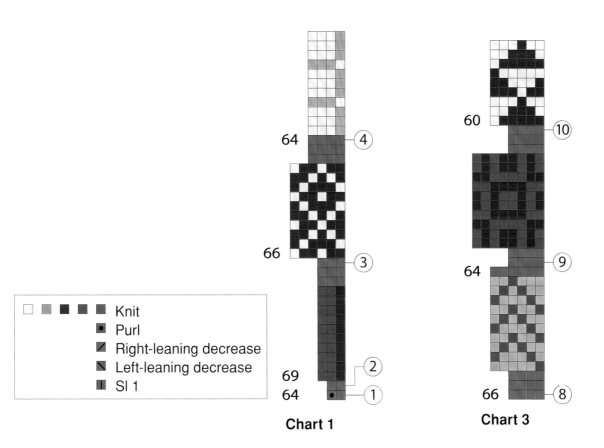

Knit
● Purl
◨ Right-leaning decrease
◧ Left-leaning decrease
▮ Sl 1

Chart 1

Chart 3

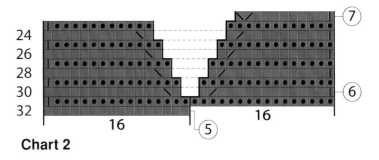

Chart 2

RASPBERRY SOCKS

MATERIALS

Yarn: CYCA #1 (sock/ fingering/baby) Sandnes Garn Sisu (80% wool, 20% nylon; 191 yd/ 175 m / 50 g): one ball each White, Bright Pink, and Green
Needles: U.S. size 1.5 / 2.5 mm: set of 5 dpn

The colors in these socks are as luscious as fresh-picked raspberries. Wear them on a cold, dark winter's day and you'll be walking on sunshine! These socks are also perfect for wearing in the early summer—because, really, who says wool socks can only be worn in winter?

Instructions:

① With Green, CO 70 sts and divide sts onto 4 dpn; join. The rounds begin at the side of the sock. Work following Chart 1, repeating the pattern around. The first 6 rounds make a narrow lace edging.

② On the round with the encircled 2, increase 2 sts evenly spaced around = 72 sts.

③ After completing rows of Chart 1, follow Chart 2 for the heel: K35 sts; turn and p35. Place the 37 rem sts on a holder for the instep (you'll come back to these sts when the heel is finished). Work back and forth over the 35 heel sts until you've repeated the 4-row pattern 4 times for the heel = 4 stripes of each color.

④ Shape the heel by decreasing at center back on every other row as shown on the chart.

⑤ On the last heel row, work 8 sts and then decrease 3 times as shown on the chart. Cut yarn, leaving a long enough tail of Green for grafting. Fold the heel in half and join the two sets of 11 sts each with Kitchener st.

⑥ Now work following Chart 3 for the foot.
Rnd 1: Pick up and knit 17 sts along each side of the heel, increase 1 st before the instep and then work the 37 instep sts in pattern. The pattern (with its charted decreases) is repeated 6 times around.

⑦ Decrease as indicated on the chart = 66 sts rem.

⑧ **Toe Shaping:** Begin at the encircled 8 and decrease as shown on the chart.

⑨ Cut yarn and draw end through rem sts; tighten. Weave in all ends neatly on WS.

Make the second sock the same way.

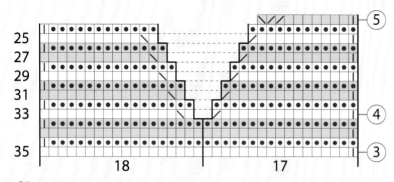

Chart 2

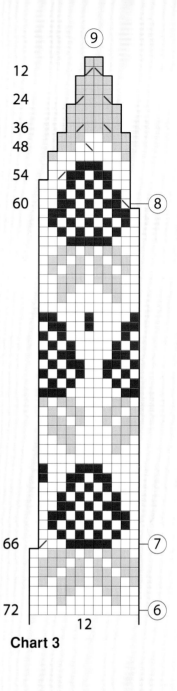

Chart 3

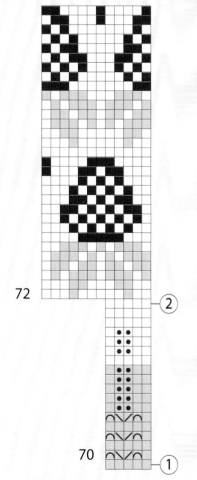

Chart 1

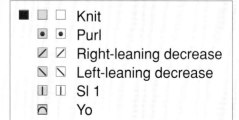

			Knit
			Purl
			Right-leaning decrease
			Left-leaning decrease
			Sl 1
			Yo

OWLS

These socks are worked in a straight-forward and easy manner and should be made with a sturdy, high-quality sock yarn.

MATERIALS

Yarn: CYCA #2 (sport/baby) Dale Garn Falk (100% wool; 116 yd/106 m / 50 g): 2 balls each Charcoal and Gray-white + a small amount of Red for the stripe at the top of the leg

Needles: U.S. size 2.5 / 3 mm: set of 5 dpn

When evening falls, the owls wake up and check to see if there is anything to eat. Even in the weak light of the stars, they can see everything that moves down on the ground, no matter how small!

Instructions:

① With Gray-white, CO 60 sts and divide sts evenly onto 4 dpn; join. The rounds begin at the side of the sock. Work following Chart 1, repeating the pattern around.

② After completing rows of Chart 1, follow Chart 2 for the heel: K30 sts; turn and p30. Place the 30 rem sts on a holder for the instep (you'll come back to these sts when the heel is finished). Work back and forth over the 30 heel sts until you've worked 14 rows.

③ Shape the heel by decreasing at center back on every other row as shown on the chart.

④ On the last heel row, work 8 sts and then decrease 2 times as shown on the chart. Cut yarn, leaving a long enough tail for grafting. Fold the heel in half and join the two sets of 10 sts each with Kitchener st.

⑤ Now work following Chart 3 for the foot.
Rnd 1: Pick up and knit 15 sts along each side of the heel and then work the 30 instep sts in pattern.

⑥ After completing Chart 3, continue on to Chart 4.

⑦ **Toe Shaping:** Try on the sock and begin shaping toe if foot is desired length. If you follow the chart, the toe will be 2 in / 5 cm from the start of the decreasing to the tip of the toe. If you decrease on every other round, the shaping will be narrower, with about 3½ in / 9 cm between the first decrease round and the tip of the toe.

⑧ Cut yarn and draw end through rem sts; tighten. Weave in all ends neatly on WS.

Make the second sock the same way.

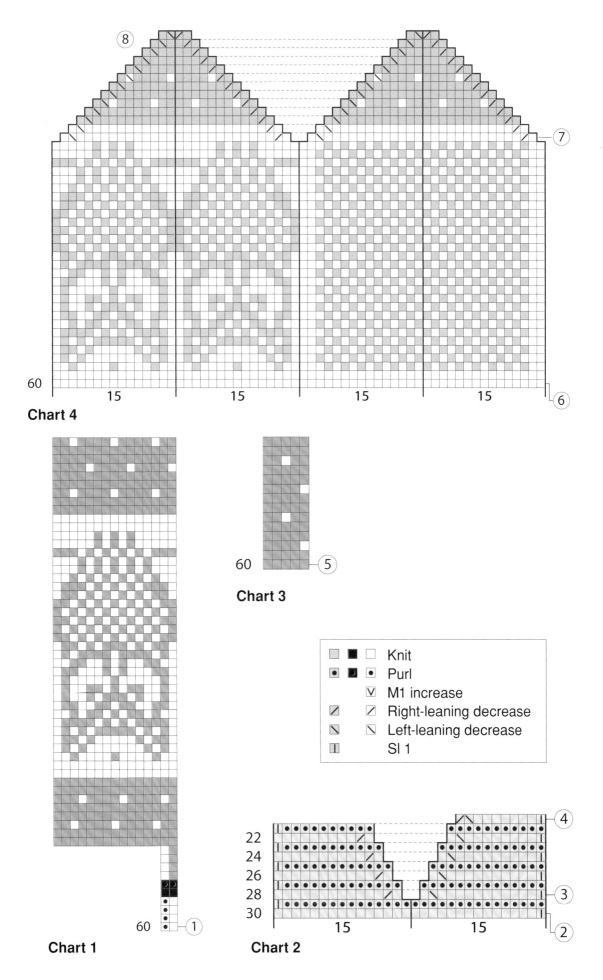

Chart 4

Chart 3

		Knit
•	◐	Purl
	∨	M1 increase
◩	◪	Right-leaning decrease
◩	◣	Left-leaning decrease
⫿		Sl 1

Chart 1

Chart 2

CAT
AND MOUSE

MATERIALS

Yarn: CYCA #1 (sock/fingering/baby) Sandnes Garn Sisu (80% wool, 20% nylon; 191 yd/ 175 m / 50 g): one ball each Turquoise, Purple, and White

Needles: U.S. size 1.5 / 2.5 mm: set of 5 dpn

The irritated cat and impudent mouse are each on their own sock which is for the best. The socks have long legs with fun patterning and a panel for a name, so it's easy to find the owner if the socks go astray.

Instructions:

① With Purple, CO 66 sts and divide sts onto 4 dpn; join. The rounds begin at the center back of the sock. Work following Chart 1, repeating the pattern around.

② At the encircled 2, decrease 2 sts evenly spaced around = 64 sts rem.

③ After completing Chart 1, work following Chart 2, the name panel. Draw in the letters (see the example above Chart 3). Place the letters so that the name is centered on the chart.

④ Work Chart 3.

⑤ Continue to Chart 4 for the heel: Cut yarn. The heel is worked back and forth over the 32 sts at center back. Begin 16 sts before the beginning of the round. Repeat the 4-row pattern 4 times so there are 4 stripes of each color.

⑥ Decrease at center back of the heel on every other row as shown on the chart.

⑦ On the last heel row, work 8 sts and then decrease 2 times as shown on the chart. Cut yarn, leaving a long enough tail for grafting. Fold the heel in half and join the two sets of 10 sts each with Kitchener st.

⑧ Now work following Chart 6 or 7 for the foot. **Rnd 1:** Pick up and knit 16 sts along each side of the heel and then work the 32 instep sts in pattern.

⑨ **Toe Shaping:** Continuing in charted pattern, shape toe as shown on the chart.

⑩ Join the sets of sole and instep sts with Kitchener st. Weave in all ends neatly on WS.

Make the second sock the same way, changing the animal on the foot.

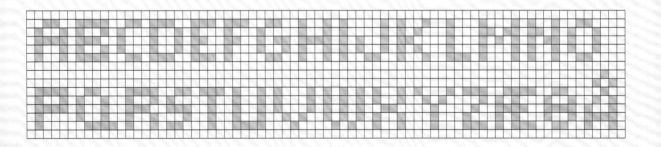

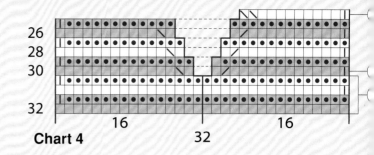

Chart 4

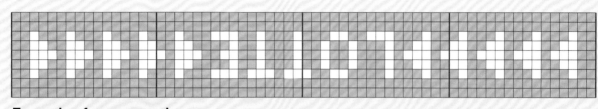

Example of name panel

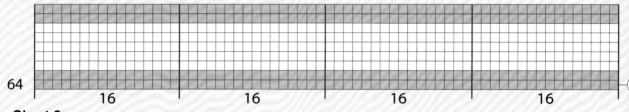

Chart 2

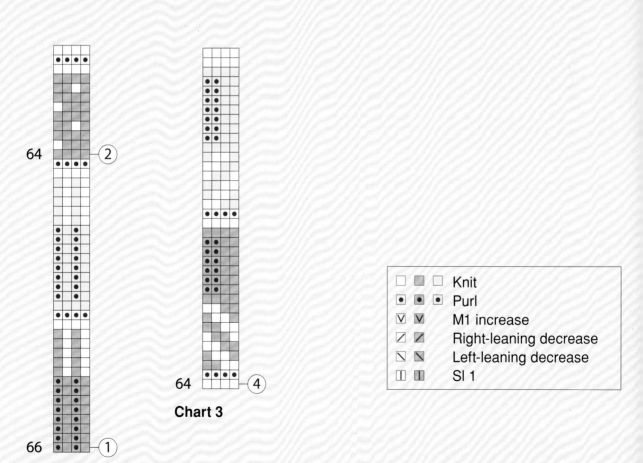

Chart 1

Chart 3

			Knit
●	●	●	Purl
Ⅴ	Ⅴ		M1 increase
◺	◿		Right-leaning decrease
◼	◼		Left-leaning decrease
◫	◫		Sl 1

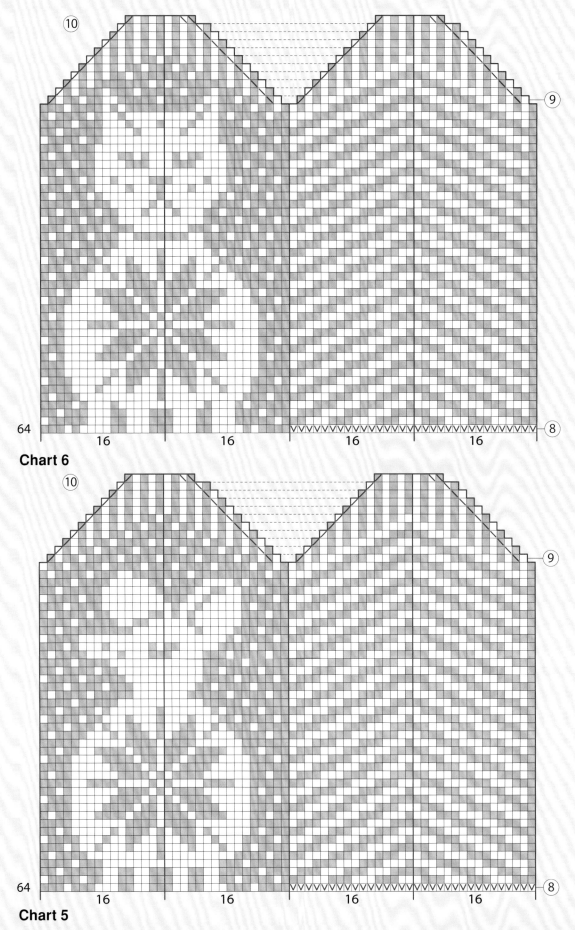

Chart 6

Chart 5

THE SOUTH POLE

MATERIALS

Yarn: CYCA #1 (sock/fingering/baby) Sandnes Garn Sisu (80% wool, 20% nylon; 191 yd/ 175 m / 50 g): one ball each Turquoise, White, and Black

Needles: U.S. size 2.5 / 3 mm: set of 5 dpn

Life at the South Pole can be wonderful, at least if you are a penguin. In this case, the penguins stand upright, lined up on the edge of the ice to relax, all warm and cozy in their down and feathers. Below the ice, the sea is brimming with fish, so the evening meal is guaranteed.

Instructions

① With White, CO 56 sts and divide sts onto 4 dpn; join. The rounds begin at the side of the sock. Work following Chart 1, repeating the pattern around. Repeat the first rnd of k2, p2 ribbing for 8 rnds.

② At the encircled 2, increase 4 sts evenly spaced around = 60 sts.

③ At the encircled 3, increase 4 sts evenly spaced around = 64 sts.

④ After completing Chart 1, work following Chart 2 for the heel: K32, turn and p32. Place the 32 rem sts on a holder for the instep (you'll come back to these sts when the heel is finished).

⑤ Repeat the 4 rows indicated by the encircled 5 4 times = 4 stripes of each color.

⑥ Decrease at center back of the heel on every other row as shown on the chart.

⑦ On the last heel row, work 9 sts and then decrease 2 times as shown on the chart. Cut yarn, leaving a long enough tail of Turquoise for grafting. Fold the heel in half and join the two sets of 11 sts each with Kitchener st.

⑧ Now work following Chart 3 for the foot.
Rnd 1: Pick up and knit 18 sts along the right side of the heel and 19 sts on the left side and then work the 32 instep sts in pattern = 69 sts. The fish pattern is marked with horizontal white lines for each repeat to make it easier to follow. The drawing of the fish motif shows one repeat.

⑨ At the encircled 9, decrease 1 st on each side of the sole as shown on the chart. Decrease again on every 3rd rnd until 63 sts rem.

⑩ At the encircled 10, decrease one st on this round as shown on the chart.

⑪ **Toe Shaping:** Continuing patterns, shape toe as shown on the chart.

⑫ Join the sets of sole and instep sts with Kitchener st. Weave in all ends neatly on WS.

Make the second sock the same way.

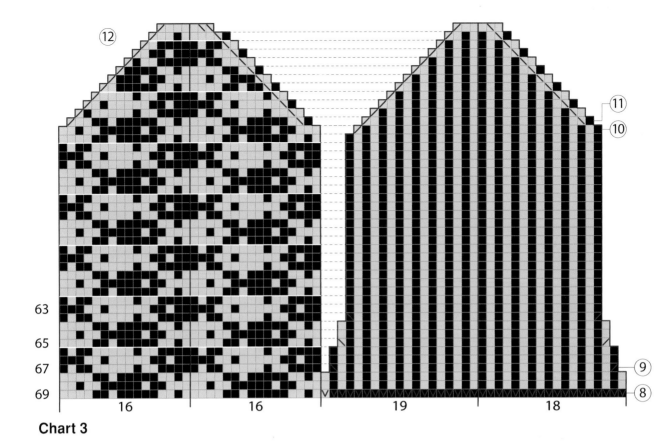

Chart 3

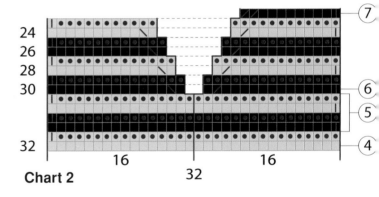

Chart 2

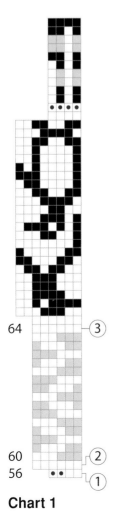

Chart 1

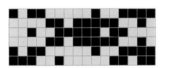

Fish Pattern

☐ ■ ▧		Knit
⊡		Purl
▨		M1 increase
◪ ◪		Right-leaning decrease
◪ ◪		Left-leaning decrease
▮ ▯		Sl 1

SNOWFLAKES

MATERIALS

Yarn: CYCA #1 (sock/fingering/baby) Viking of Norway Nordlys (75% wool, 25% nylon; 382 yd/ 349 m / 100 g): one 100 g ball each Blue #927 and White
Needles: U.S. sizes 1.5 and 2.5 / 2.5 and 3 mm: sets of 5 dpn
Gauge: 27 sts = 4 in / 10 cm
Foot Length: The foot length corresponds to women's shoe size U.S. 5½-6½ / Euro 36-37 (short) or U.S. 7½-8½ / Euro 38-39 (long). These socks can be worked in several adult sizes (see the table at the beginning of this chapter).

On extra cold days, when the snow crunches under the soles of your shoes and your breath frosts as it comes out of your mouth, you can see such pretty snowflakes. The pattern for the socks was inspired by such a winter's day.

Instructions:

NOTE: You'll need two sizes of double-pointed needles for these socks. Use the larger dpn for the sections with two-color stranded knitting and the smaller needles for the sections with only a single color.

① With smaller dpn and Blue, CO 68 sts and divide sts evenly onto 4 dpn; join. The rounds begin at the side of the sock. Work following Chart 1, repeating the pattern around. Repeat the first chart row with k1, p1 ribbing for 11 rounds.

② At the encircled 2, increase 1 st on each needle to 72 sts. Change to larger dpn.

③ At the encircled 3, decrease a total of 6 times with 11 sts between each decrease = 66 sts rem.

④ Repeat the 2 rnds marked by the encircled 4 six times (= 12 rnds total) =
Rnd 1: Knit.
Rnd 2: K1, p1.

⑤ Now work from Chart 2, noting that the pattern is not the same all the way around.

⑥ Decrease 1 st at each side as shown on the chart at encircled 6.

⑦ Turn work and p31. Place the 31 rem sts on a holder for the instep (you'll come back to these sts when the heel is finished). Do not cut the White yarn.

⑧ Repeat these 2 rows at the encircled 8 until you've worked back and forth in stockinette for a total of 21 rows.

⑨ Decrease at the center back of the heel on every other row as shown on the chart.

⑩ On the last heel row, work 7 sts and then decrease 3 times as shown on the chart. Cut yarn, leaving a long enough tail of Turquoise for grafting. Fold the heel in half and join the two sets of 10 sts

each with Kitchener st.

⑪ Continue on to Chart 3 for the foot:
Rnd 1: Pick up and knit 21 sts along the right side of the heel and 22 sts on the left side. Knit the held 31 instep sts.

⑫ At the encircled 12, begin decreasing 1 st at each side on every other rnd as shown on the chart.

⑬ Now work following Chart 4.

⑭ Repeat the rows marked by the encircled 14 2 times.

⑮ **Toe Shaping:** Decrease as indicated on the chart.

⑯ Join the sets of sole and instep sts with Kitchener st. Weave in all ends neatly on WS.

Make the second sock the same way.

		Knit
●	●	Purl
	Ⅴ	Increase 1 with M1
☑	☑	Right-leaning decrease
☒	☒	Left-leaning decrease
Ⅱ		Sl 1

Chart 1

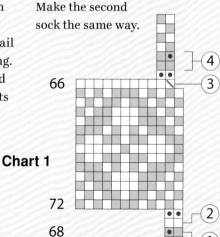

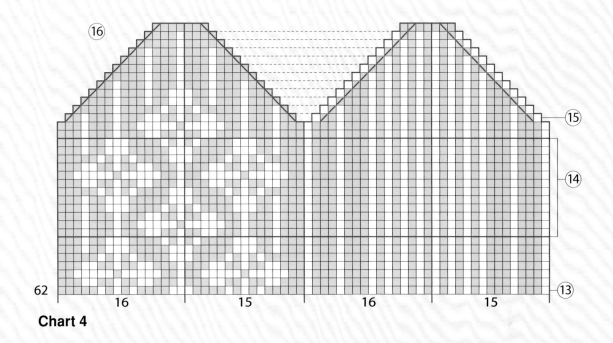

Chart 4

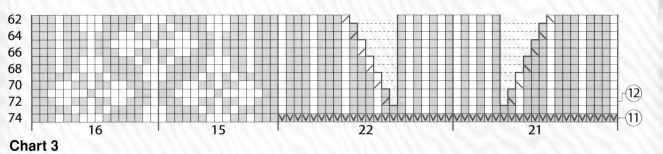

Chart 3

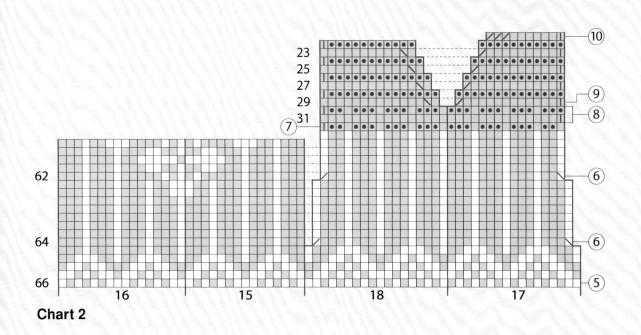

Chart 2

LET'S ROCK

MATERIALS

SMALL SIZE
Yarn: CYCA #1 (sock/fingering/
baby) Viking of Norway Nordlys
(75% wool, 25% nylon; 382 yd/ 349 m
/ 100 g): one 100 g ball each Black,
White, and Multicolor #949 (enough
for 2 pairs of socks)
Needles: U.S. size 2.5 / 3 mm: set of
5 dpn

LARGE SIZE
Yarn: CYCA #3 (DK/light worsted) Du Store
Alpakka Sterk (40% Merino wool, 40% al-
paca, 20% nylon; 150 yd/137 m / 50 g): two
balls each of Black and White
Needles: U.S. size 4 / 3.5 mm: set of 5 dpn

Here are the perfect socks for rockin' feet!
If you like strong rhythms, rock-and-roll,
and groovy piano riffs, these socks are
designed especially for you.

Instructions:

① With Black, CO 60 sts and divide sts evenly onto 4 dpn; join. The rounds begin at the side of the sock. Work following Chart 1, repeating the pattern around.

② At the encircled 2, increase 1 st on each needle to 64 sts.

③ At the encircled 3, repeat the round of k2, p2 ribbing 10 times.

④ Now work following Chart 2 for the heel. Begin by working the first 37 sts of round. Place the 27 rem sts on a holder for the instep (you'll come back to these sts when the heel is finished). Work back and forth in two-row stripes until there are 4 stripes of each color.

⑤ Decrease at the center back of the heel on every other row as shown on the chart.

⑥ On the last heel row, work 10 sts and then decrease 3 times as shown on the chart. Cut yarn, leaving a long enough tail for grafting. Fold the heel in half and join the two sets of 10 sts each with Kitchener st.

⑦ Continue on to Chart 3 for the foot:

Rnd 1: Beginning at right side of heel, pick up and knit 37 sts across heel. Knit the held 27 instep sts. Arrange the sts on the dpn as shown on Chart 3. Continue in pattern beginning on chart row 2.

⑧ At the encircled 8, shape toe as shown on the chart.

⑨ Join the sets of sole and instep sts with Kitchener st. Weave in all ends neatly on WS.

Make the second sock the same way.

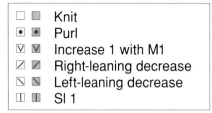

	Knit
	Purl
	Increase 1 with M1
	Right-leaning decrease
	Left-leaning decrease
	Sl 1

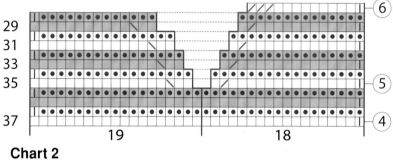

29
31
33
35
37

19   18

Chart 2

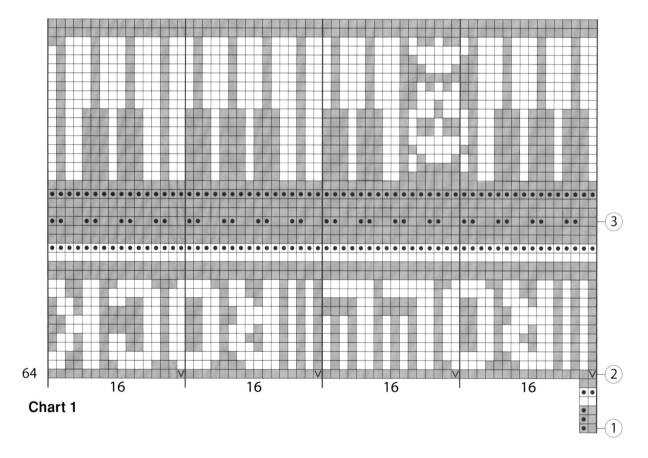

64

16   16   16   16

Chart 1

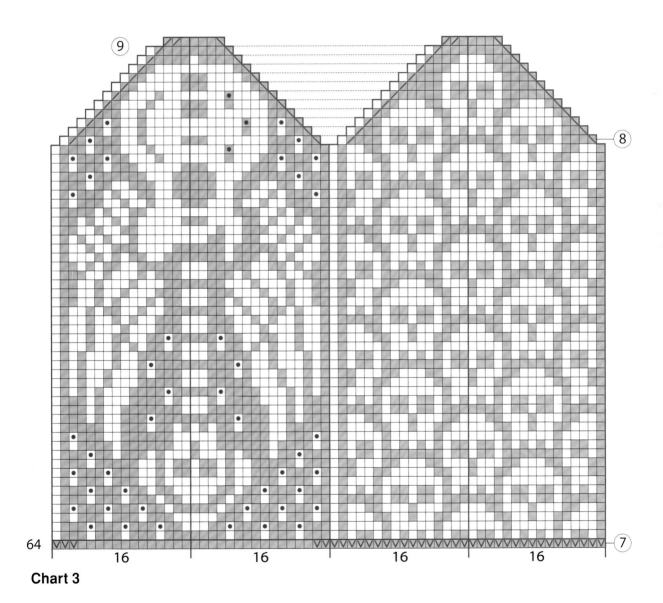

Chart 3

THICK, WARM
RUSSELESTA
RUSSIAN SOCKS

The first pattern-knitted socks I saw were of this type. The patterns showed up in weekly magazines and were knitted with unusual, ostentatious motifs, completely different from the motifs I was familiar with on Norwegian sweaters, caps, and mittens. As the name implies, the socks came from Russia.

Russian socks are knitted with two or more colors, with patterns throughout.

The most distinctive feature of these socks is their construction. Russian socks are most often knitted straight down, with the same stitch count from the cast-on edge up to the toe. Even if the foot that goes into the sock is not the same circumference all the way down, these elastic socks will shape well to the foot and fit snugly.

The heel is also special. It's set up the same way as a straight thumbhole on a mitten. A length of waste yarn is knitted where the heel will be, and when the rest of the sock is finished, this yarn is removed and the heel knitted around and around the opening where it was.

This makes it easy to arrange the pattern around the heel, and the sock will be the same thickness and be equally warm over the entire piece—the side is knitted with two strands in pattern.

Because these socks aren't knitted to fit, it's important that they not be knitted too tightly. If they're too tight, there will be too much stress around the heel when the sock is taken off.

Description and Construction Methods for Russian Socks:

The entire sock is knitted in the round, including the heel. The sock is knitted straight from the cuff to the toe. The only thing you have to remember is to knit in a strand of smooth, contrast color waste yarn where the heel will be knitted in later.

On the charts, the placement for this waste yarn is marked with a heavy horizontal line. Find a length of leftover yarn that contrasts strongly with the working yarn so you'll be able to see it clearly after you knit it in. This yarn is only a "holding" thread in the knitting.

Knit until you are beginning the first stitch above the heavy line. Drop the working yarn and use the waste yarn to knit over the stitches marked by the heavy line. Cut the waste yarn, leaving enough of a tail on each end so it won't pull out of the stitches. Push both ends of the waste yarn to the wrong side. Slide the waste yarn stitches back to the left needle.

Now pick up the working yarn and work in pattern across the waste yarn as if nothing had happened.

Finish knitting the sock and fasten off.

Heel: Insert double-pointed needles into the stitches below and above the waste yarn and carefully remove the waste yarn so you don't drop any stitches. Once the waste yarn is removed, there will be a hole where the heel will be worked around. Half of the stitches (on the sole) will be upside down when the waste yarn is removed. Make sure these stitches sit correctly on the needle as for knit stitches so your work will be as neat and even as possible.

Begin at the side and knit the stitches for the underside of the foot (sole)—the stitches that are upside down in relation to the new round. Check the chart and your stitches to make sure the stitch counts match.

Knit the heel in the round, shaping it as shown on the chart.

It is likely that there will be a little hole at each side of the heel in the transition between the leg and sole. Tighten these holes with the yarn ends and then weave them in.

RUSSIAN SOCKS
FOR LITTLE FEET

Decorate baby's feet with socks that have cute patterns and happy colors. Here are some Russian socks that even the smallest child will appreciate. The socks can't be tried on before they're finished because the heel is worked last. So the measurements of the heel are included in the table below (as measured at the center down the sole). That should make it easier to calculate the sizing of the socks.

FOOT LENGTH	HEEL LENGTH	SHOE SIZE	YARN	NEEDLES	GAUGE IN 4 IN / 10 CM
U.S. 4¼-5¼ in	1 in	4½-7	Baby yarn	1.5	28-30 sts
Euro 11-13.5 cm	2.5 cm	20-23		2.5 mm	
U.S. 5½-6¾ in	1¼ in	8-11½	Fine Sock	1.5-2.5	26-27 sts
Euro 14-17 cm	3 cm	24-29		2.5-3 mm	
U.S. 7-7½ in	1½ in	12½-1	Heavy Sock	1.5-2.5	24-25 sts
Euro 18-19 cm	3.5 cm	30-32		2.5-3 mm	
U.S. 8-8½ in	1 5/8 in	2-4½	Extra	2.5-4	22-23 sts
Euro 20-21.5 cm	4 cm	33-35	Heavy Sock	3-3.5 mm	

LITTLE BIRD

MATERIALS

Yarn: CYCA #1 (sock/fingering/baby) Dale Garn Babyull (100% Merino wool; 180 yd/165 m / 50 g): 1 ball each Bright Pink and Natural White

Needles: U.S. size 1.5 / 2.5 mm: set of 5 dpn

Foot Length: approx. 4¾ in / 12 cm; width approx. 3¼ in / 8 cm.

The socks are knitted following the chart for a small sock. If you want socks about ¾ in / 2 cm longer, use the chart for the large size.

A little bird has landed on each sock where they sit and sing a little love duet. A heart hovers over each bird as a symbol of peace and love.

Instructions:

① With Pink, CO 46 sts and divide sts onto 4 dpn; join. The rounds begin at the side of the sock. Work following Chart 1, repeating the first 6 rnds 4 times.

② **Eyelet Rnd** (see encircled 2 on Chart 1): You can omit the eyelets if you don't want ties for the socks.

③ Now work following Chart 2 (size large) or Chart 3 (small size). Increase 6 sts on the first rnd spaced as shown on the chart.

④ **Waste yarn for heel:** K3 and then knit the next 23 sts with smooth, contrast color waste yarn. Slide the 23 sts back to left needle and work in pattern.

⑤ For both sizes, continue from the encircled 5 on Chart 3.

⑥ At the encircled 6, begin toe shaping by decreasing 2 sts at each side as shown on the chart.

⑦ Join the sets of sole and instep sts with Kitchener st. Weave in all ends neatly on WS.

⑧ **Heel:** Insert a dpn into the 23 sts below the waste yarn and another dpn into the 23 sts above the waste yarn. Carefully remove waste yarn and make sure sts sit correctly on needles. Work around following Chart 5, repeating the chart twice around (the top and bottom of the heel are identical). On the first rnd, pick up and knit 2 sts at each side as shown on the chart = 50 sts total.

⑨ Shape heel by decreasing at each side as shown on the chart.

⑩ Cut yarn and draw end through rem sts; tighten. Weave in all ends neatly on WS.

Make the second sock the same way, but reverse the direction the bird faces following Chart 4.

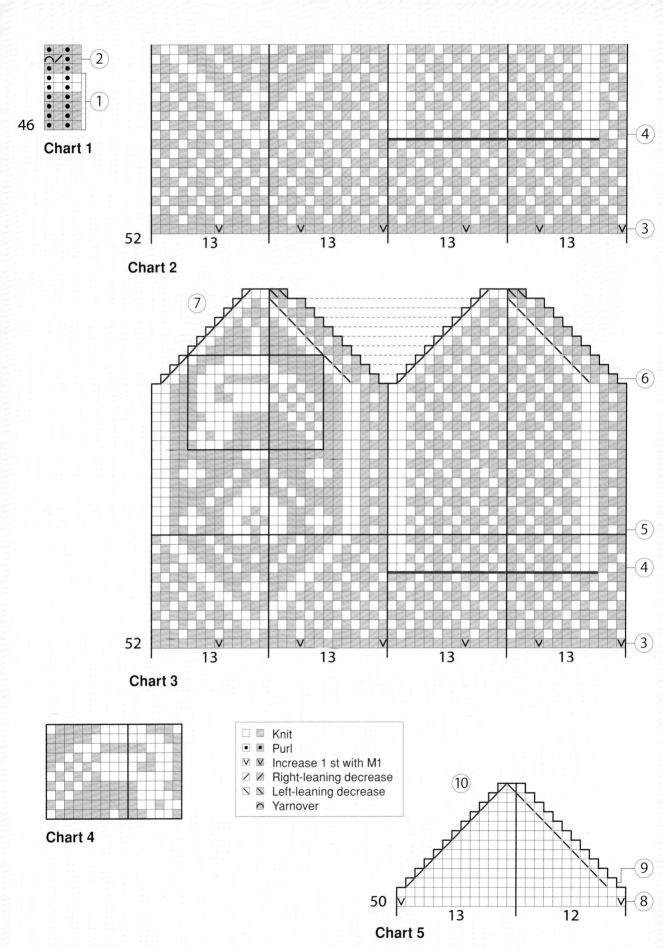

Chart 1

46

Chart 2

52   13   13   13   13

Chart 3

52   13   13   13   13

Chart 4

Knit
Purl
Increase 1 st with M1
Right-leaning decrease
Left-leaning decrease
Yarnover

Chart 5

50   13   12

LITTLE COW

MATERIALS

Yarn: CYCA #1 (sock/fingering/baby) Dale Garn Daletta (100% wool; 153 yd/140 m / 50 g): 1 ball each White, Black, and Light Green + a small amount of pink for embroidery in duplicate stitch after the knitting is finished.

Needles: U.S. size 1.5 / 2.5 mm: set of 5 dpn
Gauge: 24 sts in two-color stranded knitting = 4 in / 10 cm
Foot Length: 7-10¼ in / 18-26 cm

A real live cow can be both huge and scary for a little one. Socks with pictures of little cows with pink ears are much safer. The cow stands and looks a little to the side because she's happy to be out on the green grass.

Instructions:

① With White, CO 44 sts and divide sts onto 4 dpn; join. The rounds begin at the side of the sock. Work following Chart 1, repeating pattern around.

② At the encircled 2, increase 4 sts (inc 1 st on each needle) = 48 sts.

③ At the encircled 3, increase 4 sts (inc 1 st on each needle) = 52 sts.

④ **Waste yarn for heel** (at encircled 4): K1 and then knit the next 25 sts with smooth, contrast color waste yarn. Slide the 25 sts back to left needle and work in pattern.

⑤ Work the pattern panel at the encircled 5 for about ⅜ in / 1 cm. If you want a shorter or longer foot, adjust the number of of rounds with green stripes at this point.

⑥ Now work following Chart 2.

⑦ At the encircled 7, begin toe shaping by decreasing 2 sts at each side as shown on the chart.

⑧ Join the sets of sole and instep sts with Kitchener st. Weave in all ends neatly on WS.

⑨ **Heel** (Chart 3): Insert a dpn into the 25 sts below the waste yarn and another dpn into the 25 sts above the waste yarn. Carefully remove waste yarn and make sure sts sit correctly on needles.

Work around following Chart 3, repeating the chart twice around (the top and bottom of the heel are identical). On the first rnd, pick up and knit 1 st at each side as shown on the chart = 52 sts total.

⑩ Shape heel by decreasing at each side as shown on the chart.

⑪ Seam heel as for toe.

⑫ Weave in all ends neatly on WS. Use the pink yarn and a blunt tapestry needle to embroider the ears and muzzle on the cow with duplicate stitch.

Make the second sock the same way.

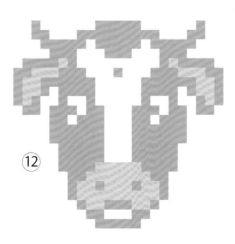

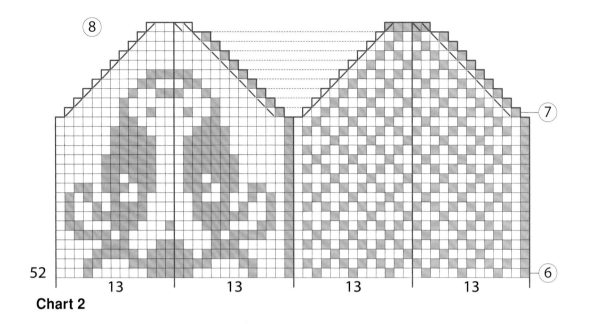

Chart 2

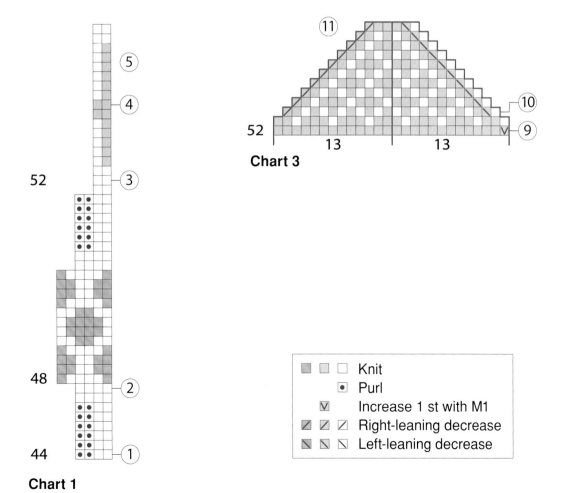

Chart 3

Chart 1

■	■	□	Knit
	●		Purl
	Ⅴ		Increase 1 st with M1
◩	◪	⬕	Right-leaning decrease
◨	◨	⬔	Left-leaning decrease

LITTLE RABBIT

MATERIALS

Yarn: CYCA #1 (sock/fingering/baby) Sandnes Garn Sisu (80% wool, 20% nylon; 191 yd/ 175 m / 50 g): one ball each Pink and White

Needles: U.S. size 1.5 / 2.5 mm: set of 5 dpn

Gauge: 34 sts in two-color stranded knitting = 4 in / 10 cm

Foot Length: 4¾ (5½) in / 12 (14) cm

The sweet rabbit with a big heart shows its front and back on these socks. The cute paws on the sock soles will certainly inspire an extra spring in the steps of the wearer.

Instructions:

① With White, CO 48 sts and divide sts onto 4 dpn; join. The rounds begin at the side of the sock. Work following Chart 1, repeating pattern around.

② At the encircled 2, repeat the 4 rows 4 times = 4 stripes of each color. Work to end of Chart 1.

③ Now begin working from Chart 2, increasing 4 sts on the first rnd as shown on the chart = 52 sts.

④ **Waste yarn for heel** (at encircled 4): K2 and then knit the next 25 sts with smooth, contrast color waste yarn. Slide the 25 sts back to left needle and work in pattern.

⑤ Continue following Chart 2 for one sock and, for the other, work the section indicated by encircled 5 following Chart 3 so the rabbit is shown from both sides.

⑥ At the encircled 6, begin toe shaping by decreasing 2 sts at each side as shown on Charts 2 and 3 respectively. When Chart 3 is completed for the second sock, follow top of Chart 2 for the rest of the sock.

⑦ Join the sets of sole and instep sts with Kitchener st. Weave in all ends neatly on WS.

⑧ **Heel** (Chart 4): Insert a dpn into the 25 sts below the waste yarn and another dpn into the 25 sts above the waste yarn.

Carefully remove waste yarn and make sure sts sit correctly on needles. Work around following Chart 4, beginning at the arrow (the underside of the foot). The light stitches below it show the rounds that have already been worked. Pick up and knit 1 st at each side on the first rnd as shown on the chart = 52 sts around.

⑨ Decrease two sts at each side as shown on the chart.

⑩ Seam the heel as for the toe. Weave in all ends neatly on WS.

Make the second sock the same way except for the sections of the rabbit/paws on the instep/sole (see step 5).

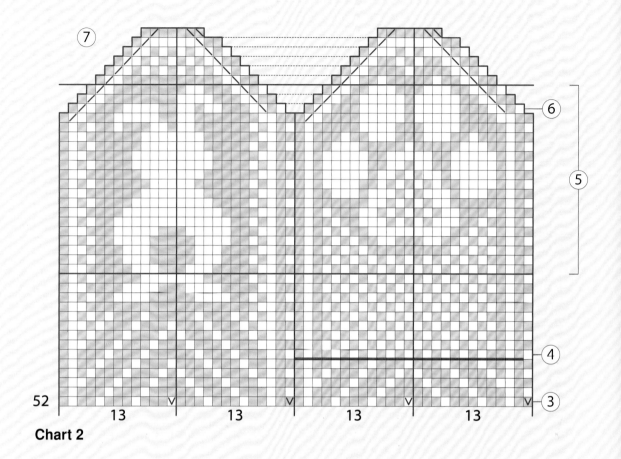

Chart 2

52

13   13   13   13

Chart 1

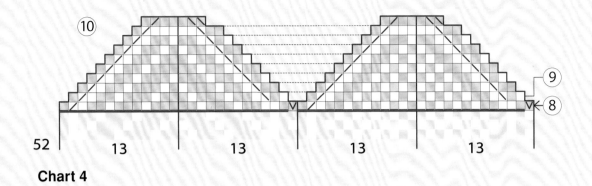

⑩

52

13   13   13   13

Chart 4

9

8

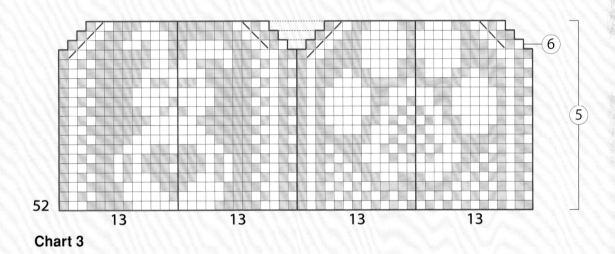

6

5

52

13   13   13   13

Chart 3

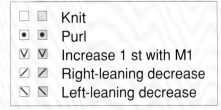

		Knit
•	•	Purl
V	V	Increase 1 st with M1
⟋	⟋	Right-leaning decrease
⟍	⟍	Left-leaning decrease

RUSSIAN SOCKS
FOR BIGGER FEET

Cat or dog? Fish or bird? Or, maybe a pair of dancing elephants in an elegant embrace? You can knit socks that will precisely match the recipient's preferences, with choices of animals, graphic patterns, and colors.

All the socks in this section are designed to fit a women's shoe size about U.S. size 6½-7½ / Euro 37-38. The yarn and needles were chosen for each pattern to yield these sizes.

Choose yarn and needles that will work together to produce the gauge you need for a given size. The socks cannot be tried on until they are finished since the heel is knitted last. For that reason, the chart below has the heel length added (as measured under the foot), to make it easier to calculate the finished sock size.

FOOT LENGTH	HEEL LENGTH	SHOE SIZE	YARN	NEEDLES	GAUGE IN 4 IN / 10 CM
U.S. 8¾-9 in **Euro** 22-23 cm	1½ in 3.5 cm	5½-6½ 36-37	Fine Sock	2.5 3 mm	28-30 sts
U.S. 9½-9¾ in **Euro** 24-25 cm	1¾ in 4 cm	7½ -9½ 38-40	Fine Sock	2.5-4 3-.5 mm	26-27 sts
U.S. 10¼-10¾ in **Euro** 26-27 cm	1⅝ in 4.5 cm	10½-10* 41-43	Heavy Sock	4 3.5 mm	24-25 sts
U.S. 11-11 ¾ in **Euro** 28-30 cm	2 in 5 cm	10*-13* 44-46	Heavy Sock	4-6 3.5-4 mm	22-23 sts

Men's size; all other sizes are women's

RUSSIAN
BLOCK PATTERN

MATERIALS

Yarn: CYCA #3 (DK/light worsted) Du Store Alpakka Sterk (40% Merino wool, 40% alpaca, 20% nylon; 150 yd/137 m / 50 g): one ball each Black, Light Purple, Light Green, and Pink. You can also work the pattern with only two colors as shown on the chart.

Needles: U.S. size 2.5 / 3 mm: set of 5 dpn

The patterning for these Russian block socks has been arranged with a variety of filler motifs and might bring to mind a quilt. On one of the socks, the heel is worked "on the other side" or you can make them both alike.

Instructions:

① With Black, CO 64 sts and divide sts onto 4 dpn; join. The rounds begin at the side of the sock. Work following Chart 1 which shows all 64 sts around.

② **Waste yarn for heel** (at encircled 2): K1 and then knit the next 31 sts with smooth, contrast color waste yarn. Slide the 31 sts back to left needle and work in pattern. **NOTE:** The heel sts with waste yarn are shown on the right side of the chart for one sock and on the left side for the second sock so that the socks will have different patterns on the instep and sole.

③ Calculate how long of a sock you need. If you want to make the socks longer, continue from Chart 3.

④ At the encircled 4, begin toe shaping by decreasing 2 sts at each side as shown on the chart.

⑤ Join the sets of sole and instep sts with Kitchener st. Weave in all ends neatly on WS.

⑥ **Heel** (Chart 3—the heel is the same on both socks): Insert a dpn into the 31 sts below the waste yarn and another dpn into the 31 sts above the waste yarn. Carefully remove waste yarn and make sure sts

sit correctly on needles. Work around following Chart 3, beginning at the underside of the foot. Pick up and knit 1 st at each side on the first rnd as shown on the chart = 64 sts around.

⑦ Decrease two sts at each side as shown on the chart.

⑧ Seam the heel as for the toe. Weave in all ends neatly on WS.

Make the second sock the same way, reversing the placement of the heel (see Step 2).

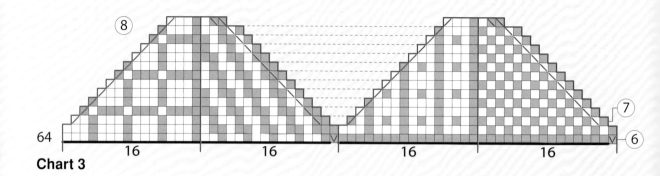

Chart 3

64 ··· 16 ··· 16 ··· 16 ··· 16

8
7
6

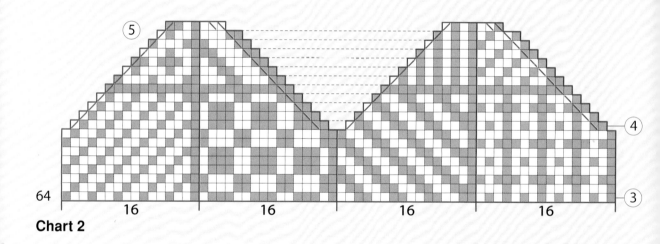

Chart 2

64 ··· 16 ··· 16 ··· 16 ··· 16

5
4
3

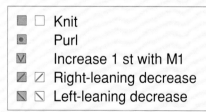

▨	☐	Knit
⊡		Purl
☒		Increase 1 st with M1
▨	☑	Right-leaning decrease
▨	☒	Left-leaning decrease

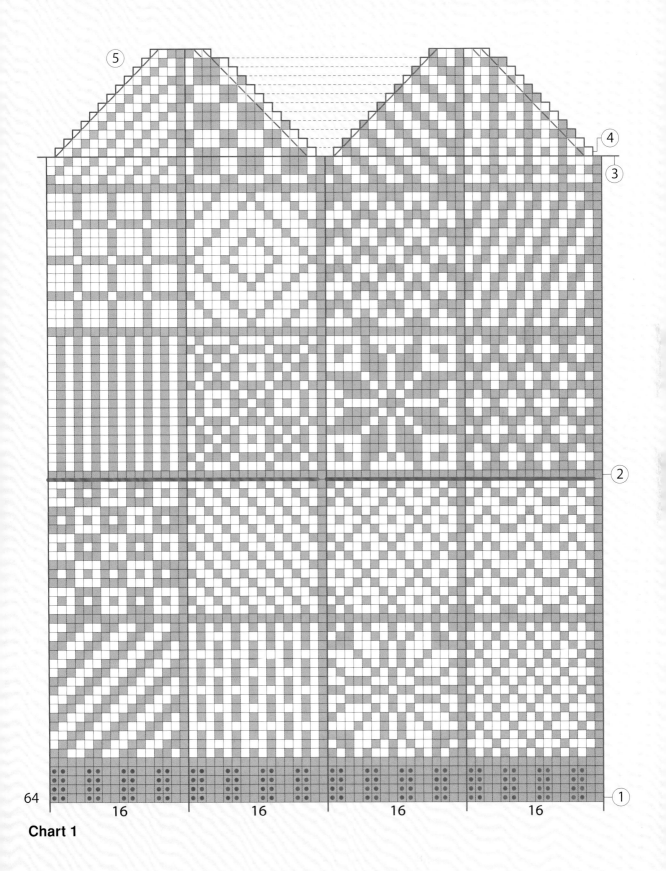

Chart 1

64

16   16   16   16

SHELL

MATERIALS

Yarn: CYCA #3 (DK/
light worsted) Du Store
Alpakka Sterk (40% Me-
rino wool, 40% alpaca,
20% nylon; 150 yd/137 m /
50 g): one ball each White
and Red

Needles: U.S. size 2.5 / 3 mm: set of 5 dpn

This special shell pattern follows the lines of the foot
and emphasizes its silhouette. The intricate little
pattern makes a wonderful effect with the stripes at
the top of the leg.

Instructions:

① With White, CO 64 sts and divide sts onto 4 dpn; join. The rounds begin at the side of the sock. Work following Chart 1, repeating the pattern around.

② Now work following Chart 2. The pattern is repeated twice around, with both sides of the sock knitted the same way. On the first rnd (at the encircled 2), decrease 1 st each at front and back as shown on the chart = 62 sts rem.

③ At the encircled 3, increase 1 st on each side = 64 sts.

④ **Waste yarn for heel** (at encircled 4): K1 and then knit the next 31 sts with smooth, contrast color waste yarn. Slide the 31 sts back to left needle and work in pattern.

⑤ Calculate how long of a sock you need. If you want to make the socks longer, continue from Chart 3.

⑥ At the encircled 6, begin toe shaping by decreasing 2 sts at each side as shown on the chart. On the last round, decrease 3 sts on each side.

⑦ Join the sets of sole and instep sts with Kitchener st. Weave in all ends neatly on WS.

⑧ **Heel** (Chart 4): Insert a dpn into the 31 sts below the waste yarn and another dpn into the 31 sts above the waste yarn. Carefully remove waste yarn and make sure sts sit correctly on needles. Begin at the arrow (the light sts shown below it have already been knitted). On the first round, pick up and knit 1 st at each side as shown on the chart = 64 sts around.

⑨ Decrease two sts at each side as shown on the chart. On the last round, decrease 3 sts each on top and bottom of heel.

⑩ Seam the heel as for the toe. Weave in all ends neatly on WS.

Make the second sock the same way.

Chart 1

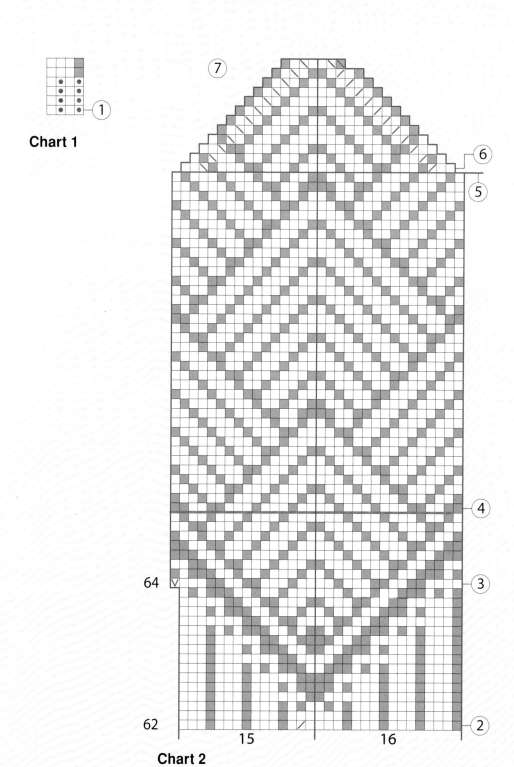

Chart 2

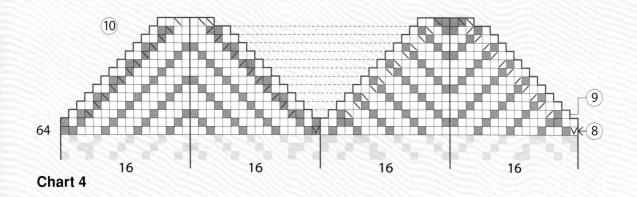

Chart 4

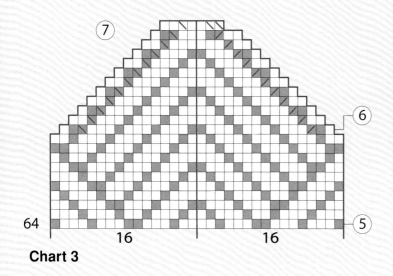

Chart 3

▨ ☐	Knit	
	•	Purl
▨ ⩔	Increase 1 st with M1	
▨ ◿	Right-leaning decrease	
▨ ◺	Left-leaning decrease	

RUSSIAN ROSE

MATERIALS

Yarn: CYCA #3 (DK/light worsted) Du Store Alpakka Sterk (40% Merino wool, 40% alpaca, 20% nylon; 150 yd/137 m / 50 g): one ball each Dark Rose and Light Rose

Needles: U.S. size 2.5 / 3 mm: set of 5 dpn

This pretty flower pattern is easy to memorize and looks great on the socks. Knit the flowers in two shades of rose, as shown, or choose two different colors that coordinate well. The striped heel is a fun contrast to the flowers.

Instructions:

With Dark Rose (or darker color), CO 60 sts and divide sts onto 4 dpn; join. The rounds begin at the side of the sock. Work around in k2, p2 ribbing for 4 rnds and then knit 2 rnds. On the last rnd, increase 4 sts evenly spaced around = 64 sts.

Now work following Chart 1, repeating the pattern 4 times around. Work in pattern until leg is about 4¾ in / 12 cm long.

Waste yarn for heel: K1 and then knit the next 31 sts with smooth, contrast color waste yarn. Slide the 31 sts back to left needle and work in pattern.

Continue in pattern until the foot is long enough before the toe shaping. Calculate the foot length from the gauge of the knitting already done. The heel and toe, together, will measure the same as the length of 25 rnds. You can calculate the length on the foot from the waste yarn to the heel shaping from this.

Chart 2: The pattern is repeated twice around for the top and bottom of the sock foot, both of which are worked alike. Decrease at the sides of the foot as shown on the chart.

Join the sets of sole and instep sts with Kitchener st. Weave in all ends neatly on WS.

Heel (Chart 3): Insert a dpn into the 31 sts below the waste yarn and another dpn into the 31 sts above the waste yarn. Carefully remove waste yarn and make sure sts sit correctly on needles. Work following Chart 3, beginning the round so the sole is worked first. On the first round, pick up and knit 1 st at each side as shown on the chart = 64 sts around.

Decrease two sts at each side as shown on the chart. On the last round, decrease 3 sts each on sole and instep.

Seam the heel as for the toe. Weave in all ends neatly on WS.

Make the second sock the same way.

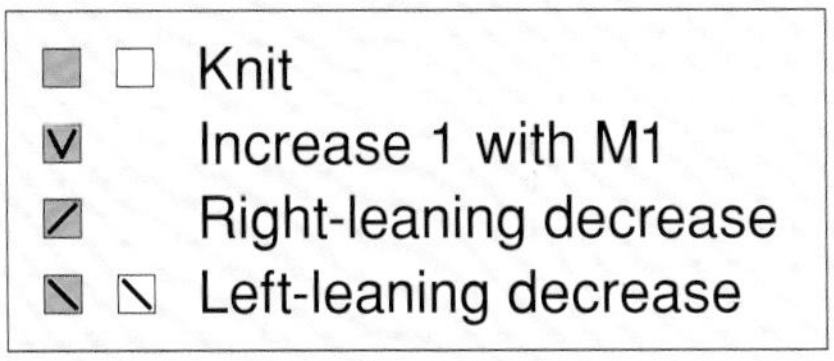

Knit
Increase 1 with M1
Right-leaning decrease
Left-leaning decrease

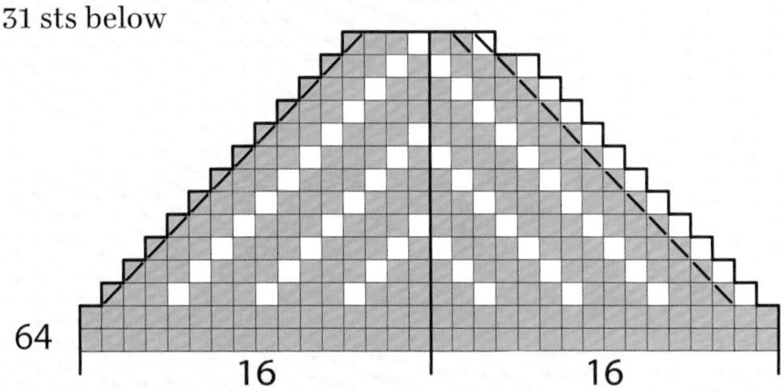

64
16
16

Chart 2

64

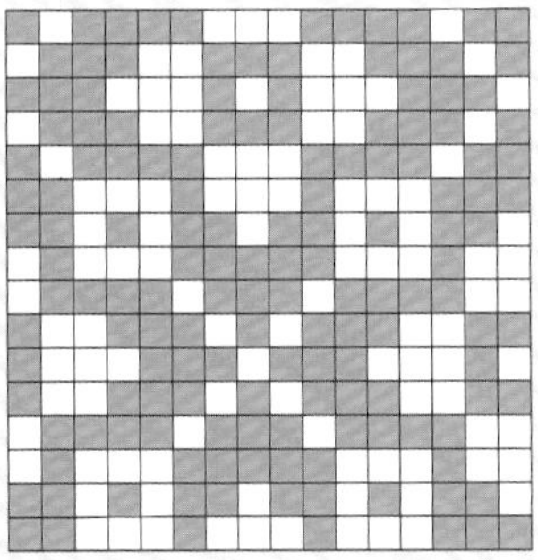

Chart 1

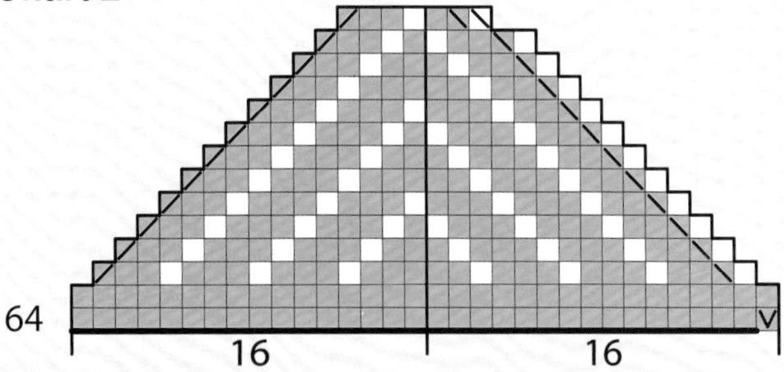

64
16
16

Chart 3

TANGO-ELEPHANTS

MATERIALS

Yarn: CYCA #3 (DK/light worsted) Du Store Alpakka Sterk (40% Merino wool, 40% alpaca, 20% nylon; 150 yd/137 m / 50 g): one ball each White and Blue

Needles: U.S. size 2.5 / 3 mm: set of 5 dpn

Large elephants are actually very graceful, as you can see from the silhouettes here. These enamored elephants have found their rhythm in an intense tango as they sway together, blowing soap bubble hearts with their trunks.

Instructions:

① With White, CO 60 sts and divide sts onto 4 dpn; join. The rounds begin at the side of the sock. Work 4 rnds of k1, p1 ribbing.

② Now work following Chart 1. On the first rnd, increase 4 sts evenly spaced around as shown on the chart = 62 sts rem.

③ Work the section marked by the encircled 3 three times total.

④ **Waste yarn for heel** (at encircled 4): K1 and then knit the next 30 sts with smooth, contrast color waste yarn. Slide the 30 sts back to left needle and work in pattern.

⑤ At the encircled 5, begin toe shaping by decreasing 2 sts at each side as shown on the chart.

⑥ Join the sets of sole and instep sts with Kitchener st. Weave in all ends neatly on WS.

⑦ **Heel** (Chart 2): Insert a dpn into the 30 sts below the waste yarn and another dpn into the 30 sts above the waste yarn. Carefully remove waste yarn and make sure sts sit correctly on needles. Work following Chart 2, beginning at the arrow. (The light stitches below the dark red line indicate the rounds already worked.) The round begins with the sole On the first rnd, pick up and knit 2 sts at each side as shown on the chart = 64 sts total. Beginning on the 2nd rnd, decrease 2 sts at each side as indicated on the chart.

⑧ Seam the heel as for the toe. Weave in all ends neatly on WS.

Make the second sock the same way.

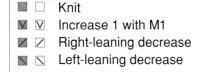

■	□	Knit
☑	☑	Increase 1 with M1
◪	☑	Right-leaning decrease
◪	◩	Left-leaning decrease

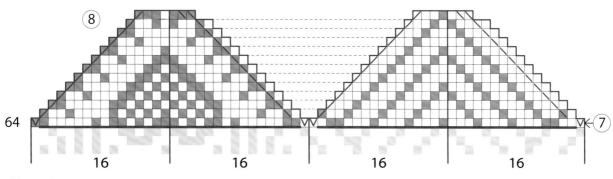

Chart 2

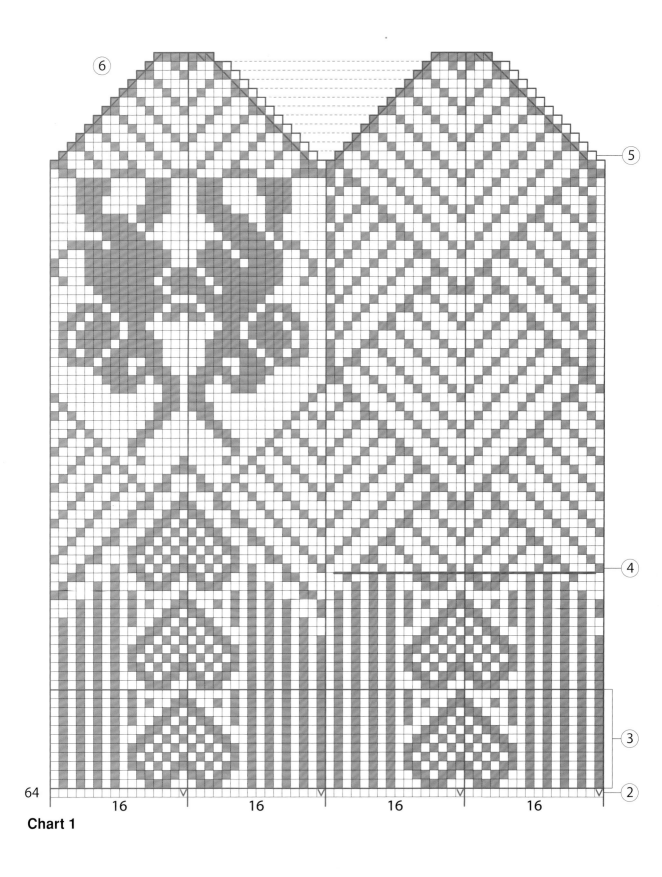

Chart 1

CAT

MATERIALS

Yarn: CYCA #3 (DK/light worsted) Du Store Alpakka Sterk (40% Merino wool, 40% alpaca, 20% nylon; 150 yd/137 m / 50 g): one ball each Dark Green, White, and Red

Needles: U.S. size 2.5 / 3 mm: set of 5 dpn

These cats have just eaten a big meal of fish, but they are already hunting high and low for even more food. Their elegantly swishing tails are mirrored in the panel at the top of the leg and their footprints are on the sock soles.

Instructions:

① With Dark Green, CO 56 sts and divide sts onto 4 dpn; join. Work following Chart 1, beginning with 12 rnds of k2, p2 ribbing (encircled 1).

② At the encircled 2, increase 4 sts evenly spaced around = 60 sts; continue in pattern to end of Chart 1.

③ Now work following Chart 2.

④ **Waste yarn for heel** (at encircled 4): Knit the first 29 sts with smooth, contrast color waste yarn. Slide the 29 sts back to left needle and work in pattern.

⑤ At the encircled 5, begin toe shaping by decreasing 2 sts at each side as shown on the chart.

⑥ After completing charted rows, join the sets of sole and instep sts with Kitchener st. Weave in all ends neatly on WS.

⑦ **Heel** (Chart 3): Insert a dpn into the 29 sts below the waste yarn and another dpn into the 29 sts above the waste yarn. Carefully remove waste yarn and make sure sts sit correctly on needles. Work following Chart 3, beginning with the sole (at the arrow and encircled 7). The light sts underneath are sts already knitted.) On the first rnd, pick up and knit 1 st at each side as shown on the chart = 60 sts total. Beginning on the 2nd rnd, decrease 2 sts at each side as indicated on the chart.

⑧ Seam the heel as for the toe. Weave in all ends neatly on WS.

Make the second sock the same way.

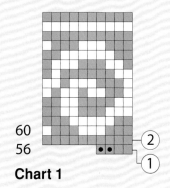

60
56

Chart 1

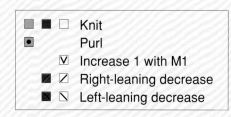

▨	■	☐	Knit
	⊡		Purl
		☑	Increase 1 with M1
◤	◪		Right-leaning decrease
◣	◩		Left-leaning decrease

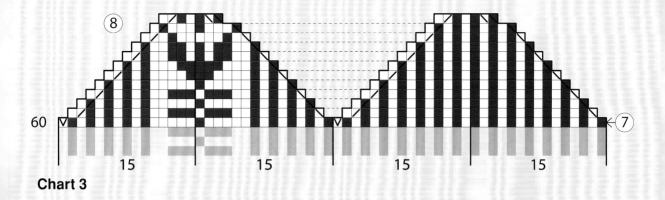

Chart 3

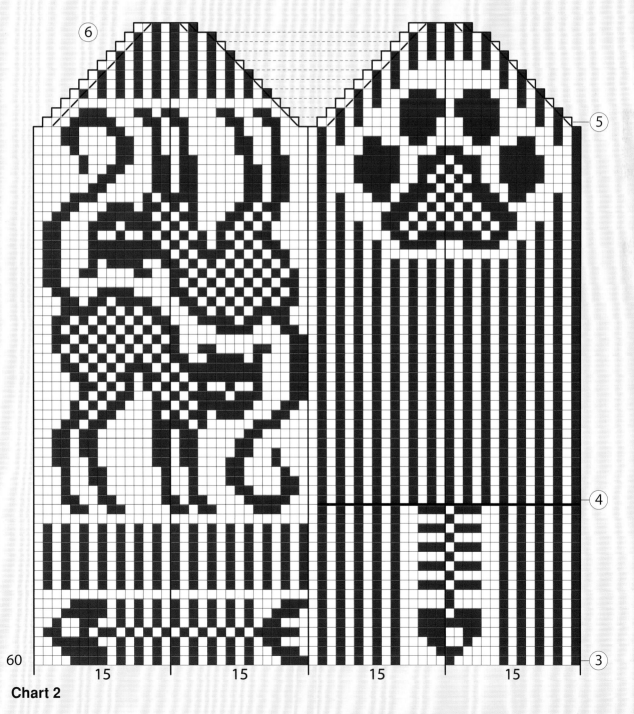

Chart 2

DOG

MATERIALS

Yarn: CYCA #2 (sport/baby) Dale Garn Falk (100% wool; 116 yd/106 m / 50 g): 1 ball Black and 2 balls Light Gray Heather

Needles: U.S. size 2.5 / 3 mm: set of 5 dpn

Dog lovers also need good socks. The dogs on these socks do not like cats. One frightened cat is up the tree and the other is hiding behind the heel. Cute dog bones embellish the sock legs and, of course, dog paws are on the soles.

Instructions:

① With Black, CO 56 sts and divide sts onto 4 dpn; join. Work following Chart 1, beginning with 8 rnds of k1, p1 ribbing (encircled 1).

② At the encircled 2, increase 4 sts evenly spaced around = 60 sts; continue in pattern to end of Chart 1.

③ Repeat the charted row at the encircled 3 10 times.

④ Now work following the respective Chart 2 for left or right foot.

⑤ **Waste yarn for heel** (at encircled 4): Knit the first 29 sts with smooth, contrast color waste yarn. Slide the 29 sts back to left needle and work in pattern.

⑥ Work the rounds indicated by the encircled 6. Don't forget to work the respective right or left sock so the dogs will face each other.

⑦ At the encircled 7, begin toe shaping by decreasing 2 sts at each side as shown on the chart.

⑧ After completing charted rows, join the sets of sole and instep sts with Kitchener st. Weave in all ends neatly on WS.

⑨ **Heel** (Chart 4 or 5): Insert a dpn into the 29 sts below the waste yarn and another dpn into the 29 sts above the waste yarn. Carefully remove waste yarn and make sure sts sit correctly on needles.

Work following Chart 4 or 5 for the right or left sock, beginning with the sole. (The light sts underneath are sts already knitted.) On the first rnd, pick up and knit 1 st at each side as shown on the chart = 60 sts total.

⑩ Decrease 2 sts at each side as shown on the chart.

⑪ Seam the heel as for the toe. Weave in all ends neatly on WS.

Make the second sock the same way, working from mirror-image charts.

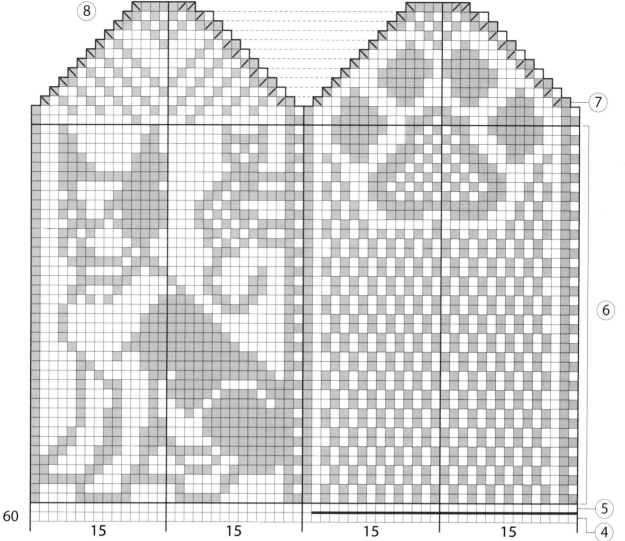

Chart 2 (right sock)

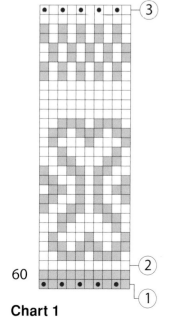

Chart 1

		Knit
⊡	⊡	Purl
☑		Increase 1 with M1
◪	◿	Right-leaning decrease
◪	◹	Left-leaning decrease

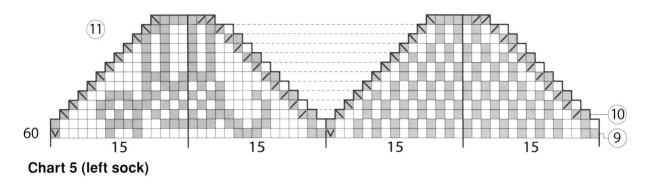

11

60

15 15 15 15

10
9

Chart 5 (left sock)

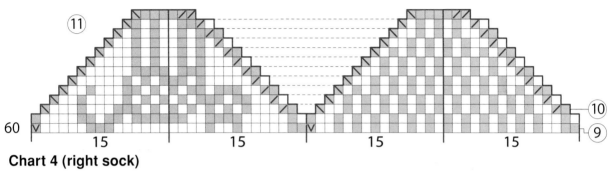

11

60

15 15 15 15

10
9

Chart 4 (right sock)

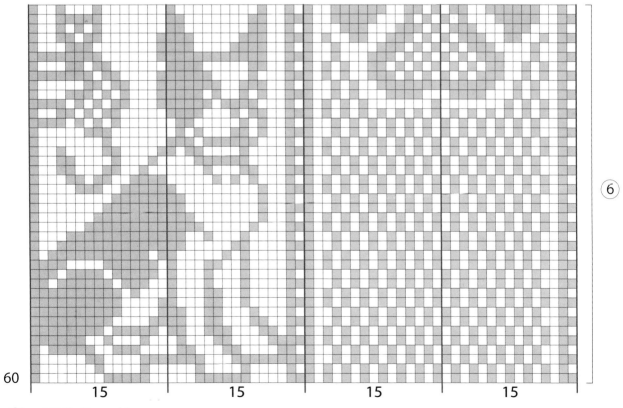

6

60

15 15 15 15

Chart 3 (left sock)

The photo shows socks with Norwegian words; the chart has been updated with English.

SHIP AHOY

MATERIALS

Yarn: CYCA #3 (DK/light worsted) Du Store Alpakka Sterk (40% Merino wool, 40% alpaca, 20% nylon; 150 yd/137 m / 50 g): two balls Navy Blue and 1 ball White; a small amount each of Red and Green to embroider on the lanterns at the back of the heels.

Needles: U.S. size 2.5 / 3 mm: set of 5 dpn

These socks are designed as an aid for anyone who is the captain of her or his own ship. On the front of the sock, you'll see a Selbu rose functioning as a compass. The socks are marked with the starboard and port sides and feature the correct lantern colors. The four white stripes on the sock legs correspond to the stripes of a captain's uniform.

Instructions:

① With Black, CO 60 sts and divide sts onto 4 dpn; join. Work following Chart 1, beginning with 16 rnds of k2, p2 ribbing (encircled 1).

② Repeat the chart rows marked by the encircled 2, 3 times and then complete Chart 1.

③ Now work from Chart 2, increasing 4 sts on the first rnd as shown on the chart = 64 sts.

④ **Waste yarn for heel** (at encircled 4): K1 and then knit the next 31 sts with smooth, contrast color waste yarn. Slide the 31 sts back to left needle and work in pattern.

⑤ At the encircled 5, work the text of Chart 2 as shown, with both socks worked the same way.

⑥ At the encircled 6, begin toe shaping by decreasing 2 sts at each side as shown on the chart.

⑦ After completing charted rows, join the sets of sole and instep sts with Kitchener st. Weave in all ends neatly on WS.

⑧ **Heel** (Chart 3): Insert a dpn into the 31 sts below the waste yarn and another dpn into the 31 sts above the waste yarn. Carefully remove waste yarn and make sure sts sit correctly on needles.

Work following Chart 3, beginning with the sole (see arrow at encircled 8). (The light sts underneath are sts already knitted.) On the first rnd, pick up and knit 1 st at each side as shown on the chart = 64 sts total.

⑨ Begin decreasing at the encircled 9.

⑩ Seam the heel as for the toe. Weave in all ends neatly on WS.

Embroider the lantern for the port side sock heel with Red and use Green for the starboard.

Make the second sock the same way, substituting the text as described in step 5.

Chart 2

7

6

5

4

3

64

16 16 16 16

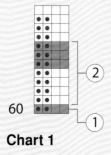

2

1

60

Chart 1

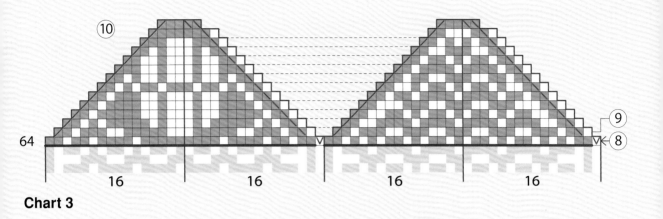

Chart 3

Port

Starboard

□	▨	Knit
⊡	▨	Purl
ⱱ	ⱱ	Increase 1 with M1
◩	◪	Right-leaning decrease
◹	◩	Left-leaning decrease

COD

Yarn: CYCA #3 (DK/light worsted) Du Store Alpakka Sterk (40% Merino wool, 40% alpaca, 20% nylon; 150 yd/137 m / 50 g): one ball each of Gray and White + a small amount of Red for the cuff stripes

Needles: U.S. size 2.5 / 3 mm: set of 5 dpn

These socks are designed for those of us who particularly appreciate a cod dinner, whether lutefisk or another other tasty dish with this excellent fish. Maybe you know a fisherman who deserves a pair of sturdy, warm socks?

Instructions:

① With Gray, CO 60 sts and divide sts onto 4 dpn; join. Work following Chart 1, repeating the pattern around.

② At the encircled 2, increase 4 sts evenly spaced around = 64 sts; complete Chart 1.

③ Now work from Chart 2 for one sock and Chart 3 for the other.

④ **Waste yarn for heel** (at encircled 4): K1 and then knit the next 30 sts with smooth, contrast color waste yarn. Slide the 30 sts back to left needle and work in pattern.

⑤ Work in pattern to the encircled 5 and then work toe shaping by decreasing 2 sts at each side as shown on the chart.

⑥ After completing charted rows, join the sets of sole and instep sts with Kitchener st. Weave in all ends neatly on WS.

⑦ **Heel** (Chart 3): Insert a dpn into the 30 sts below the waste yarn and another dpn into the 30 sts above the waste yarn. Carefully remove waste

yarn and make sure sts sit correctly on needles. Work following Chart 4, beginning with the sole (see arrow at encircled 7). (The light sts underneath are sts already knitted.) On the first rnd, pick up and knit 2 sts at each side as shown on the chart = 64 sts total.

⑧ Begin at the encircled 8, decrease 2 sts at each side as shown on the chart.

⑨ Seam the heel as for the toe. Weave in all ends neatly on WS.

Make the second sock the same way.

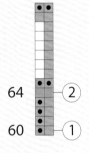

64 ⊙—②

60 ⊙—①

Chart 1

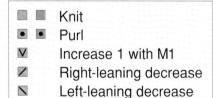

		Knit
•	•	Purl
Ⅴ		Increase 1 with M1
╱		Right-leaning decrease
╲		Left-leaning decrease

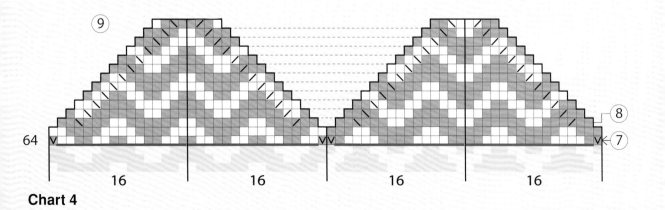

64 — ⑨ ... ⑧ ... ⑦

16   16   16   16

Chart 4

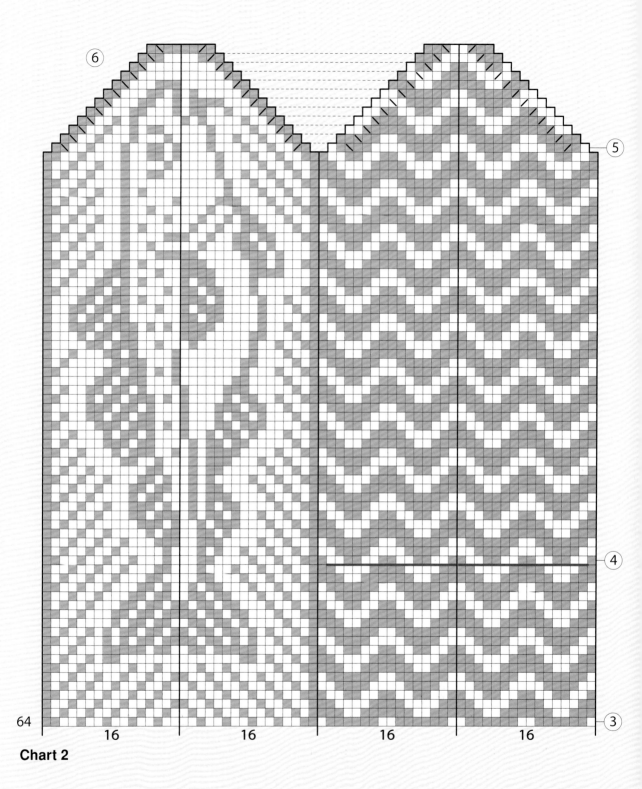

Chart 2

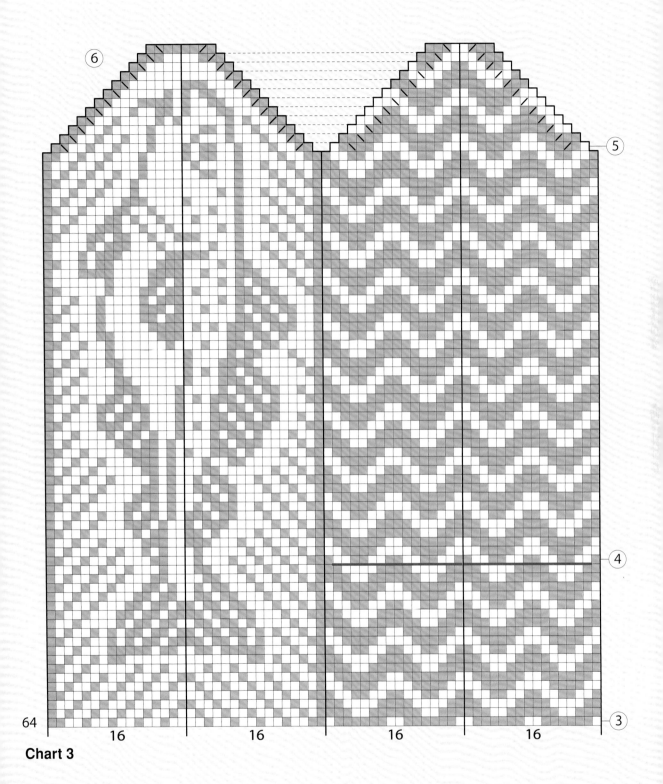

Chart 3

PTARMIGAN

MATERIALS

Yarn: CYCA #2 (sport/baby) Dale Garn Falk (100% wool; 116 yd/106 m / 50 g): 2 balls each Dark Red and White

Needles: U.S. size 2.5 / 3 mm: set of 5 dpn

The ptarmigan sit in pairs, glancing lovingly at each other. They're still in their white winter coloring. It's easy to spot the tracks of the ptarmigan in the freshly-fallen snow—and you can find them on the soles of these socks.

Instructions:

① With Red, CO 60 sts and divide sts onto 4 dpn; join. Work following Chart 1, repeating the pattern around.

② At the encircled 2, increase 4 sts evenly spaced around (= increase 1 st on each of the 4 dpn) = 64 sts; the pattern repeats twice around.

③ Work the pattern starting at the encircled 3 once around.

④ **Waste yarn for heel** (at encircled 4): K1 and then knit the next 31 sts with smooth, contrast color waste yarn. Slide the 31 sts back to left needle and work in pattern.

⑤ After completing Chart 1, work from Chart 2, decreasing 4 sts evenly spaced around as shown on the chart = 60 sts rem. The pattern is worked twice around.

⑥ At the encircled 6, begin toe shaping by decreasing 2 sts at each side as shown on the chart.

⑦ On the last round (encircled 7), with White, decrease all the rem sts. Now join the sets of sole and instep sts with Kitchener st. Weave in all ends neatly on WS.

⑧ **Heel:** Insert a dpn into the 31 sts below the waste yarn and another dpn into the 31 sts above the waste yarn. Carefully remove waste yarn and make sure sts sit correctly on needles. Work following Chart 3, beginning with the sole. (The light sts underneath are sts already knitted.) On the first rnd, pick up and knit 1 st at each side as shown on the chart = 64 sts total.

⑨ At the encircled 9, decrease 2 sts at each side as shown on the chart.

⑩ Seam the heel as for the toe. Weave in all ends neatly on WS.

Make the second sock the same way.

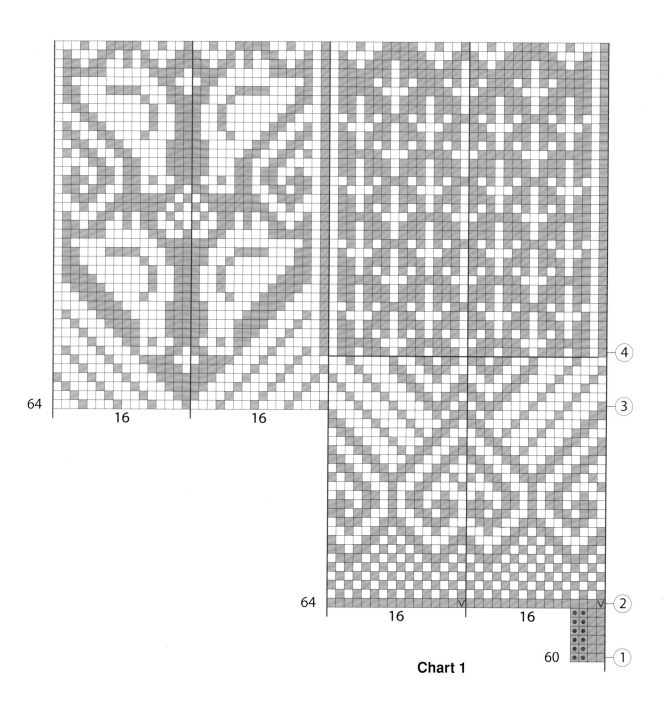

Chart 1

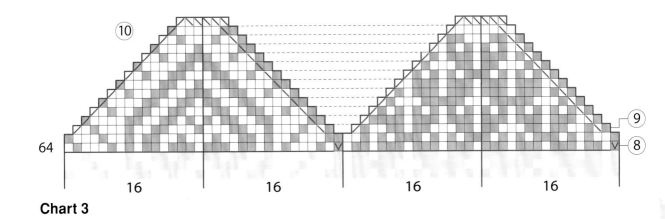

Chart 3

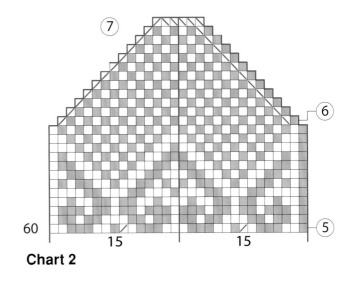

Chart 2

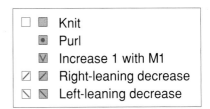

☐	▦	Knit
	⊡	Purl
	☒	Increase 1 with M1
◹	◩	Right-leaning decrease
◺	◪	Left-leaning decrease

CONVERSE SNEAKER
SOCKS

MATERIALS

Yarn: CYCA #2 (sport/baby)
Dale Garn Falk (100% wool;
116 yd/106 m / 50 g): 1 ball
Pink (as shown) or Blue (as
charted) and 2 balls White

Needles: U.S. size 2.5 / 3
mm: set of 5 dpn

Look cool even when you go out in your stocking
feet! These stylish Converse sneaker socks have
long, fold-down ribbed cuffs, and shoelaces are
embroidered on afterwards with chain stitch.
Converse sneakers come in many different colors,
so you just have to choose your or the recipient's
favorite colors to match the shoes.

Instructions:

With White, CO 52 sts and divide sts onto 4 dpn; join. Work around in k2, p2 ribbing for 20 rnds.

① Now work following Chart 1. On the first rnd, increase 13 times as shown = 65 sts. The dark horizontal lines on the chart will help you position the rounds where you will make the eyelets for the "shoelaces."

② **Waste yarn for heel** (at encircled 2): Knit the next 32 sts with smooth, contrast color waste yarn. Slide the 32 sts back to left needle and continue in pattern.

③ At the encircled 3, begin toe shaping by decreasing 2 sts at each side as shown on the chart. On the last rnd, decrease an additional stitch at the center front (see chart).

④ Now join the two sets of 9 sts each with Kitchener st. Weave in all ends neatly on WS.

⑤ **Heel:** Insert a dpn into the 32 sts below the waste yarn and another dpn into the 32 sts above the waste yarn. Carefully remove waste yarn and make sure sts sit correctly on needles. Work following Chart 2, beginning with the sole (see arrow at encircled 5). (The light sts underneath are sts already knitted.) On the first rnd, pick up and knit 3 sts as shown on the chart = 67 sts total.

⑥ Decrease 2 sts at each side as shown on the chart.

⑦ Seam the heel as for the toe. Weave in all ends neatly on WS.

Embroider on the "shoelaces" using White and chain st, working the lines from eyelet to eyelet (see photo). Do not put the laces through the top holes of the sock. Fix the opening at the side of the heel with a chain stitch so that the edge around the sole will be smooth and even.

Make the second sock the same way.

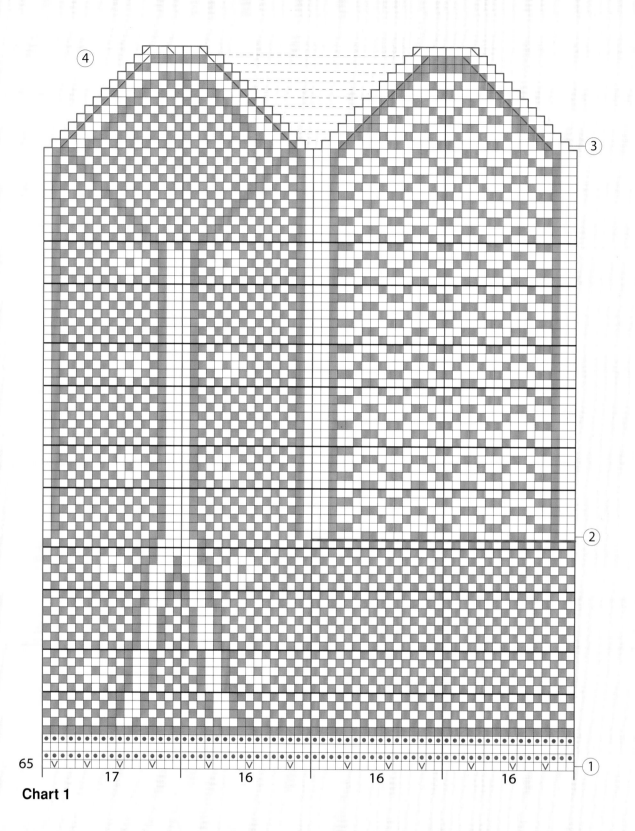

Chart 1

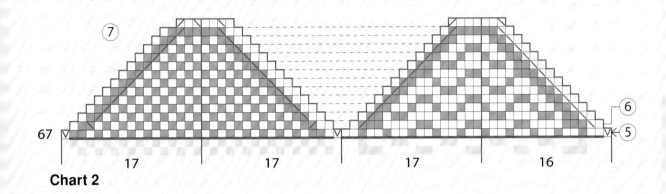

⑦

67

Chart 2

17   17   17   16

	Knit
	Purl
⩗	Increase 1 with M1
⬕ ⧄	Right-leaning decrease
⬕ ⧅	Left-leaning decrease

⑥
⑤